Indians of the Southeast

UP FROM THESE HILLS

Memories of a Cherokee Boyhood

Leonard Carson Lambert Jr.

As told to Michael Lambert

UNIVERSITY OF NEBRASKA PRESS | LINCOLN AND LONDON

© 2011 by the
Board of Regents of the
University of Nebraska
All rights reserved
Manufactured in the
United States of America
∞
Library of Congress
Cataloging-in-Publication Data

Lambert, Leonard Carson.
Up from these hills: memories of a
Cherokee boyhood / Leonard Carson
Lambert Jr.; as told to Michael Lambert.
p. cm. — (Indians of the Southeast)
Includes bibliographical references.
ISBN 978-0-8032-3536-6 (pbk.: alk. paper)
1. Lambert, Leonard Carson. 2. Cherokee
Indians—Biography. I. Lambert, Michael
C., 1960– II. Title.
E99.L26A3 2011
975.004'97557—dc22
[B]   2011012653

Set in Iowan Old Style by Kim Essman.
Designed by Ray Boeche.

Valerie, Jessica, and Hailey
for you and all who follow

Begin not by reading about South Dakota, but by looking for the Indian history beneath your own feet. | Paul Chaat Smith, *Everything You Know about Indians Is Wrong*

Contents

Leonard Lambert fits no one's stereotype of an American Indian, but the contours of Lambert's life are more typical than we might think. A well-educated professional who lived all over the world as an adult, he never permanently resided on the Cherokee reservation where he was born. Like Lambert, most American Indians do not live on reservations, and they pursue a range of occupations that were largely closed to their forebears. Also like Lambert, their identity as citizens of Native nations remains strong. In this memoir of his family and childhood, Lambert paints a vivid portrait of how he became the man he is. Born into a struggling Cherokee family on the Eastern Band reservation in western North Carolina, Lambert moved with his family to east Tennessee in the 1940s so his father could find a job as a farm laborer and secure an occupational draft deferment. The whole family worked hard, but a limited understanding of market forces and a lack of confidence in negotiating labor contracts kept them in poverty. The experience, however, broadened Lambert's horizons. Attending a public school with white children, Lambert discovered that he loved school and that he was smart. The family's subsequent move to Mars Hill, North Carolina, opened other opportunities, including the possibility of a college education. But none of these off-reservation experiences muted the family's identity as Cherokee. They visited relatives regularly and took in kin who came to stay, sometimes for months. As economic opportunities in Cherokee improved in the 1950s, most family members moved back to the reservation. Leonard's son and editor, anthropologist Michael Lambert, points out in his perceptive introduction that they felt no need to proclaim an identity as Cherokee; they simply knew who they were. No feathers necessary. The editors are pleased to include Leonard Lambert's memoir in the Indians of the Southeast series.

Theda Perdue
Michael D. Green

Forethoughts
MICHAEL LAMBERT

When I was young my father, Leonard Carson Lambert Jr., told us "poor stories" about his experiences growing up as an Indian on and near the reservation of the Eastern Band of Cherokee Indians in the mountains of western North Carolina. He told these stories to contrast the conditions in which he was raised with our comparatively comfortable upbringing. I caught glimpses of the world of his youth during our annual visits to my grandparents who lived on the reservation. I still remember visiting their house in Birdtown in the early 1960s. It was an old small house nestled on a hillside just above the main road. I remember dodging chickens as I walked along a narrow path that went over a stream to the outhouse. I also remember the cove where my grandfather built the family home in the 1930s. It was still standing in the late 1990s, and every so often we would trek over the Oconuluftee River and follow the road up the mountainside to see it. Despite the fact that over the years additions had been made to the original house, it remained a modest structure until it was taken down in the late 1990s, essentially the same as the one my father knew when he was a boy. The home was nestled at the foot of a small cove that gently rose behind the house up the mountainside. You could still see the garden beds that once nourished my father's family. I could easily imagine my father and his siblings playing on the mountainside while my grandfather tended to cattle in the barn and my grandmother washed clothes in a washbasin in the back of the house.

The authors of this book, my father and I, are both enrolled members of the Eastern Band of Cherokee Indians. My father assembled the draft on which this book is based because he wanted, as best he could, to tell the truth about what it was like to grow up in his parents' house. He wanted to set the record straight. After my grandfather died in 1993, stories emerged that the family had succeeded because my father and his siblings were encouraged by their parents to pursue higher education. This ran counter to my father's memories. As will become apparent from the text that follows, he does credit his parents for the success of their children, but at the same time he remembers his parents as having been indifferent to the education of their children. My father, for example, remembers that his mother did not send him to school until he was eight. Later in his life my father attributed the deterioration of his relationship with his mother, in part, to her inability to forgive him for leaving the mountains of North Carolina to pursue an engineering degree at North Carolina State College. As flattering or not as the picture might be, he wanted tell the story of his parents with as much honesty as possible so that my generation of the family could more fully understand what it was like to grow up in his parents' household during the first half of the twentieth century.

I have little doubt some will take exception to the way in which the Lambert family and other individuals are characterized in this book. After my father published a letter in the *One Feather*, the newspaper of the Eastern Band of Cherokee Indians, that described his grandma Kate's involvement in bootlegging, one of his brothers felt moved to publish an apology in the *One Feather* on my father's behalf to all who might have been offended by how this revelation might have damaged the family's reputation. I must admit that I myself was not always comfortable with how he characterized some of the people in the manuscript. The only disagreement we had over my editing of the text focused on a caustic characterization that I had removed. I thought it did little to enhance the story and that there was no reason to leave it in. To my father this did not matter; in his view if he remembered it, it should be published.

Once when we were talking about some of his more caustic descriptions, I warned him that one day someone was going to write a book about him and that the portrait would not be flattering. Without pause he leaned back in his chair and said, "You know, I think that would be a good idea. You could do it, and I will help you." I know my father, and I know that he was serious. My father has no interest in preserving anyone's reputation—neither his own nor anyone else's. For him it is far more important, however uncomfortable, that the truth be told, expressing a philosophy that our reputations are crafted by what we do and not by what we hide.

Lest I make my father's manner too noble, I also know that at times he is just trying to get a rise out of people. The words "tact" and "diplomacy" are not in his vocabulary. More often than not he will casually hurl off a few comments just to see how people will respond, with little regard to consequences. There is a lot of this in this text, and knowing my father, I have little doubt that it is deliberate. I am sure that if for no other reason, my father wrote this text to provoke others by forcing them to see his childhood through his eyes, knowing full well that they would not like what they saw.

As I struggled with how his text might be received, I realized that ultimately, the story told in these pages is neither of my experience nor of anyone else's, only my father's. With that in mind I realized that neither I nor anyone else would have to write the portrait of my father. It is contained in the pages of this document. The text that my father produced was his life as seen through his eyes, and he is as much a part of this story as are the characters he describes. I encourage those who object to how he saw the early years of his life to respond to him. He would enjoy hearing from you. As for me, I have nothing but fond memories of my grandparents, and nothing that is said in this text diminishes how I think of them. If anything, this text provides a window into how textured their lives were, the challenges they faced, their moments of hope and sadness, and their triumphs and frailties. This memoir has made them all the more human to me and hopefully to my descendants. I thank my father for having given my grandparents life beyond the years that they lived through the care that he has taken in recalling, in remarkable detail, a time in their lives that would have been otherwise inaccessible to me.

When my father began assembling these materials, he intended his work for the audience of his relatives. After I read his original text, I realized that, with work, it would be of interest to a wider audience. I had just completed my first book, and I had time to undertake the task of editing and rewriting. Substantively, this text is derived from my father's memories and is based on that written document my father produced, not on oral interviews that I had with him. The materials were not selected through an interview schedule but instead were topics that my father considered important enough to remember. This book is, to paraphrase Gore Vidal, how my father remembered a period in his life, nothing more nor less.[1] This renders the text episodic with shifting themes as my father moves through different parts of his life. What was of interest to my father when he was a young boy would clearly be different from what he would be interested in as a teenager. My father was almost seventy when this was written. He has one of those rare minds that are able to recall in his old age vivid details of his youth, and the detail that he provides in this text is remarkable. It would be hard to find in archives descriptions as vivid of what it was like to live on a mountain farm or as a sharecropper's son in Tennessee in the 1930s and '40s.

While we have used the "as told to" convention to mark the voice of the main text as that of my father, this book is best viewed as an experimental collaborative ethnography for which my father has provided the raw materials that I then shaped into a story and argument about Indian experience in the twentieth century. In part my objective is to push the boundaries of anthropological conventions of ethnography. To the extent possible I have limited myself to selecting, reorganizing, and stylistic editing. Wherever appropriate I have preserved the original wording of my father's text. I have tried my best to remain true to my father's voice and mind. The only parts that I have substantively written are the opening sections on the history of the family and the Eastern Band of Cherokee Indians and the closing pages of the final chapter.

Although this book began as a family history, a wider audience will likely find interest in the fact that this family is an Indian family. All members of my father's birth family were enrolled citizens of the Eastern Band of Cherokee Indians. While there are over two hundred groups that claim to be Cherokee, the Eastern Band of Cherokee Indians is one of only three Cherokee tribes that are recognized by the federal government. Of the three only the Eastern Band is located east of the Mississippi River. The two other Cherokee tribes, the Cherokee Nation and the United Keetoowah Band of Cherokee Indians, are headquartered in Oklahoma. Prior to 1839 most Cherokees lived east of the Mississippi, mostly in northwest Georgia, but also in areas that are now part of the neighboring states of South Carolina, Alabama, Tennessee, and North Carolina, where the Cherokees established an active and prosperous society. By the early years of the nineteenth century the Cherokees had established a press, courts, and a system of government based on a written constitution and the rule of law. Even by Anglo-American standards, which probably mattered little to most Cherokees at the time, the political and social institutions of the Cherokee Nation were as, if not more, complex, sophisticated, and progressive as those of their white neighbors in the state of Georgia.

Despite this the Southern states, and in particular Georgia, pressed their claim to the land of the Cherokee people. But the Cherokee Nation would not cede this land easily, and its members actively resisted the efforts of the state of Georgia to claim their land. They hired lawyers and pursued an aggressive publicity and legal campaign to further their cause, including the seminal Supreme Court cases *Cherokee Nation v. Georgia* and *Worcester v. Georgia*, which today provide the foundation for contemporary federal Indian law.[2]

The case of *Worcester v. Georgia* was instigated by a law enacted by the state of Georgia that required that all non-Indians living on Indian land register with the state of Georgia. Samuel Worcester and Elizur Butler, missionaries who had been living among the Cherokees, refused to do so, claiming that Georgia's laws did not apply to the land of the Cherokee Nation. The Supreme Court ruled in Worcester and Butler's favor, affirming the principle that state laws "had no force" over Indian land. Today this decision is the basis for innumerable tribal legal claims and is one of the most important legal pillars that limit the jurisdiction of states over Indian land.

In the face of a possible constitutional conflict between the executive and judicial branches and the threat of a civil war over state's rights, the Court did not follow procedures to have the decisions implemented. Of course neither the state of Georgia nor President Andrew Jackson had any intention of allowing the Cherokee Nation to remain in the East anyway. Both condoned the imposition of conditions on the Cherokees, through the application of Georgia's laws, which would force the Cherokees to agree to leave their homeland for Indian Territory, now Oklahoma.

Needless to say, with the exception of a small group of Cherokees who willingly signed the removal treaty that paved the way for the relocation of the Cherokees to Indian Territory, most of the Cherokees had to be forced at the end of a bayonet to set off on the Trail of Tears—the long, arduous, and, for many, deadly journey to the West. Some, however, managed to find a way to remain in the East. Many fled and hid in the mountains, others were granted exemptions, and some presented legal arguments that, due to their social and legal status, the removal treaty did not apply to them. The Qualla Cherokees, the core group of what would later become the Eastern Band of Cherokee Indians, chose the latter strategy. They argued that, because they had accepted reservations and severed relations with the Cherokee Nation under the treaty of 1819, the removal treaty of 1835 did not apply to them. This argument, along with the inability of the U.S. government to see the removal to completion in the rugged terrain of the North Carolina Mountains, made it possible for the Eastern Cherokees to remain in their homeland.[3]

While the largest and core group of what would eventually comprise the Eastern Band of Cherokee Indians was the Qualla Indians, they were by no means the majority. For various reasons, over the years following the removal, many of the scattered Cherokees who remained in North Carolina would begin to gather in Quallatown, what is today Cherokee, North Carolina. At the time of the removal the ancestors of both of my paternal grandparents were living near what is today the North Carolina–Georgia border—well within the boundaries of the Cherokee Nation. During the mid-1800s they, like many other Cherokees, would move north to Quallatown. During the 1860s these remnants of scattered Cherokee communities would begin the political work of rebuilding the formal political institutions of governance.

There is much reason to believe that part of the explanation for the tragic removal of the Cherokee people and the splitting of the Cherokee Nation lay in the inability of the white residents of Georgia to assimilate and understand the reality of the Cherokees, preferring instead to see the

Cherokees as primitive savages rather than as a progressive people. Of course false impressions such as these have been a durable feature of Indian–non-Indian relations in the United States. In the same way that they fueled the desire of the Georgians to cleanse their state of the Indian presence in the early 1800s, they would later inform other attempts to destroy Indian political entities, such as occurred in the early years of the twentieth century when the assets of tribes were allotted to individuals under the provisions of the Dawes Act or during the mid-twentieth century when the official policy was to terminate tribes whose citizens no longer possessed "Indian traits," as defined by non-Indians. The fact is that American Indians have always had to deal with the refusal of non-Indians to see us for who we are. We have had to live in constant comparison to what Vine Deloria has referred to as the "mythical super-Indian," often with tragic consequences.[4]

Through this text my father is also writing against this mythical super-Indian, an Indian perhaps most recognizable today through the stock stereotypes of pan-Indianism, the spiritual, feathered, drumming Indian. At times hints of this Indian would seep onto the Boundary, and each time they were angrily received by my father as inauthentic and pathetic.[5] When the *One Feather* began reporting on what the paper referred to as the "sacred" hoop dance, which historically the Cherokees never performed, my father took offense at the representation of this dance as "sacred." For him, as a Christian, an authentic faith of the Eastern Cherokees, this characterization was blasphemous, and this dance certainly had never been "sacred" to the Cherokees.[6] During a tour of the Oconuluftee Indian village, a tribally owned re-creation of a mid-1700s Cherokee village, my father heard the interpreter present a soliloquy on the terrible injustice that the boarding school at Cherokee had inflicted on the Indian students. The interpreter painted a picture of Indian agents wresting children from the arms of their distraught parents so that they could be sent to the boarding school and stripped of their Indian culture. While this characterization mirrored popular stereotypes and the experience of some Indians elsewhere in Indian country, of the impact that the boarding school experience had on Indian children, it ran counter to what my father remembered of the boarding school in Cherokee. He remembers this to have been an excellent school to which many Eastern Cherokee parents would voluntarily send their children. After watching the parade of Indians festooned in Indian dress for the opening of the National Museum of the American Indian in Washington DC, my father wryly responded, "Look at all those Indians playing monkey for the white man."

In these instances my father's understanding of his experience was running head on into popular stereotypes of Indians. This is not uncommon for Eastern Cherokees, as should be readily apparent to anyone who has visited Cherokee. Prior to the 1940s the region around Cherokee was a backwater that caught the eye of no one except for those who lived in the region. After the Second World War vacationing became an integral part of middle-class American experience, and the town of Cherokee started to move out of the shadows of the Smoky Mountains. Well positioned at the eastern entrance to the Great Smoky Mountains National Park, Cherokee would become a prime tourist destination each year for thousands of Americans. For better or worse the Eastern Cherokees decided to take advantage of this by selling their "Indianness," and the Boundary was quickly blanketed by Indian kitsch—very little of which had anything to do with the Cherokees. Oversized teepees, tomahawks, and statues of loincloth-clad Indians were among the backdrop of downtown Cherokee against which "chiefs," clad in full Plains Indian regalia, would have their photographs taken with tourists who were none the wiser that this regalia had nothing to do with the Cherokees.[7]

Eastern Cherokees are acutely aware that this imagery is nothing but a fantasy designed to attract tourists. On the one hand it provides an opening for the Eastern Cherokees to distance themselves from naive tourists. My grandmother used to tell a story of a schoolteacher who came to the door of her trailer to ask her where the Indian reservation was. When my grandmother told her that she was on the reservation, the woman looked at her incredulously and asked why, if this was the reservation, there weren't any teepees. Of course the Cherokees never lived in teepees, and probably few, if any, American Indians lived in a teepee in the mid-twentieth century. Far more Indians were living in trailers. In general the Eastern Cherokees had what could only be described as a mercenary attitude toward the imagery that surrounded them. My distant relative "Chief" Henry

Lambert, a man who was allegedly the world's most pho-tographed Indian, claimed that he tried to "chief" in the clothing that was once worn by the Cherokees but found that the tourists would not pay to have their photographs taken with him. This inspired him to wear the attire of the Plains Indians, which earned him much more money. That this story is so often retold underlies the strange relation-ship that the Eastern Cherokees have forged with their stereotypes. The materiality of this relationship was most clearly underlined when Oprah Winfrey assembled a panel of Indian activists to denounce offensive Indian sports im-agery such as that presented by the Washington Redskins or the Atlanta Braves. The then–Eastern Band principal chief, Ed Taylor, was invited to be in the audience. After patiently listening to a panel of Indian activists decry the use of Indian mascots by sports teams, Chief Taylor calmly rose from the back of the audience and proudly pointed out that the Eastern Band produced the tomahawks that fans waved at Atlanta Braves home games. He said that he did not have a problem with that because the tribe was laugh-ing all the way to the bank.

While I did not grow up on the Boundary, I visited there almost every year, and I am a citizen of the Eastern Band. My understanding of Indianness and what it means to be Eastern Cherokee was very much shaped by my exposure to the Indian kitsch that so permeated the Boundary. I must admit that once you are inured to the offensiveness of the imagery, it becomes strangely comforting. Part of that com-fort might come not so much from the images themselves,

as from the way that they push Eastern Cherokee under-
standings of what it means to be Indian out of the public eye. In sharp contrast to the legions of members of the
Cherokee groups that are not federally recognized, or individuals who self-identify as Cherokee (the self-proclaimed
descendants of Cherokee princesses) — all individuals who
for whatever reason desire to be *seen* as Indian — many enrolled members of federally recognized tribes rarely go out
of their way to have others identify them as Indian. Arguably, nothing expresses Eastern Cherokee *Indian* identity
more loudly than silence.

I would imagine that most Indians who live privately as
citizens of tribes, even those who are not Eastern Cherokee, have little interest in publicly casting their own lives
in the light of comparison to the overwhelming and blind-
ing stereotypes Americans have of Indians, a problem that
Vine Deloria eloquently addresses in *Custer Died for Your
Sins* in his discussion of the mythical super-Indian. Until
recently, this was certainly true for me. Not that I would
hide my identity if asked, just that for me there was something distasteful about proclaiming this identity. The kitsch
of Cherokee instills an understanding that the tribe of the
Eastern Band is the reality, and "Indian" is little more than
an American fantasy. It made no sense to me that anyone,
Indian or non-Indian, would have any interest in identify-
ing themselves through the repertoire of ersatz symbolism
evoked by the word "Indian."

Until I entered graduate school, it never occurred to
me that there was any reason to publicly identify as In-

dian. Of course there were economic benefits; grants were available to encourage Indian students to attend graduate school. But this is not what I am referring to. In academic environments Indians run headlong into the pervasive Indian stereotypes, which sadly are not too dissimilar from the commercial imagery of the Boundary. Vine Deloria's mythical super-Indian rarely hides, and all Indians can and do recount the times they are forced to confront it. For me this was most strikingly illustrated after I was offered a fellowship to study social anthropology at Harvard University. A dean took it upon herself to call me in an effort to convince me to decline the fellowship that was designed to bring Indian students to campus. Unimpressed by the tribal enrollment documents I had provided, she did not like the idea of this fellowship going to someone who, in her opinion, was not sufficiently Indian. She seemed particularly indignant that I did not have an authentic Indian name. I did not fit the image of the Indian she wanted walking across campus. I could only deduce that she wanted some buckskin-clad Indian sporting a headdress, I guess, someone who had the same attitude as the "chiefs" who line the roads of downtown Cherokee to have their pictures taken with naive tourists. Little did she know that mine is one of the most common Eastern Band names, right behind James and Mary Smith.

Encounters such as this drove home to me what was at stake with Indian identity. Citizens of federally recognized tribes comprise less than 1 percent of the population of the United States. So small are our numbers that to call us a minority is to overstate the weight of our voice and our visibility. Outside of a few select areas that have a high density of Indians, such as Oklahoma, Arizona, or areas around Indian reservations, you don't encounter many tribal citizens. Moreover, this is a political identity and not, as most Americans mistakenly believe, a racial or cultural identity. At sight most American Indians are invisible and are most often seen to be members of other racial groups such as white, black, Hispanic, or Asian. Most Indians who are enrolled—the vast silent majority of Indians who refuse to project their identity through the prism of the mythical super-Indian—simply pass silently and invisibly through American society. It is their voices that are all too often silenced by the din of noise produced in this country about Indians. This silent Indian majority needs to become visible and reclaim for themselves what it means to be Indian. They need to forever distance Indian identity from the stock markers that are so often identified by non-Indians as Indian. And non-Indians need to completely relearn how to see Indians.

The question is how Indians can make themselves visible without parading out Plains Indian flute music or dream catchers, or other such stereotypical tropes. It is this challenge that in part attracted me to the task of working on my father's text. If what it means to be Eastern Cherokee is deeply woven into the lives of our families, there is no better way to express who we are than to provide a brief glimpse into what this family life is about. If you come to the end of this memoir and conclude that my father's story was one of successful Indian assimilation to Anglo-American culture, you will have missed the point. You will have fallen into a trap of interpreting Indian experience through the lens of a dominant culture that prefers to see Indian experience as distinct and distant from the non-Indian world that surrounds it. This is a lens that "anthropologizes" American Indian experience by delimiting it to stereotypical traits and exoticizing it, constructing it as unable to absorb new materials and creatively change, as though historicity were a privilege of everyone except Indians.[8]

The real message is simple and mundane yet unassimilated into our national psyche: Indians are people, just plain folks. This story is about a family that had roots in the North Carolina Mountains and who happened to be Indian. In fact there was and is a great deal of commonality in the lives of Indians and non-Indians in the mountains of North Carolina, as is pretty much true everywhere in this country today. As early as 1883 Wilbur Zeigler and Ben Grosscup, after visiting the North Carolina Mountains, would report that "the Indians have no towns, nor does their manner of life differ in many particulars from that of the white people among whom they reside. A stranger, unless he sees the inmates, does not distinguish an Indian cabin from a white man's, nor, with few exceptions, an Indian's little cove farm from one of its class cultivated by a white man."[9] Non–Eastern Cherokees from this part of country will find that the story told in these pages resonates with what they know of their own family histories.

Yet to say this is in no way to contradict the fact that this is a memoir of Indian experience. All of my father's immediate family (of his generation and earlier) and most of the people mentioned in the text were or are citizens of the Eastern Band of Cherokee Indians. More has probably been written about the Cherokees than any other Indian tribe. Some of the written material is very good indeed. Some of it, however, is not, resting instead on the flimsy foundation of caricatures and stereotypes. This work attempts to go beyond the latter by presenting portraits of real individuals and their experiences. In the text that follows my father and I have attempted, to the best of our abilities, to accurately represent the experiences of one Eastern Cherokee family as they struggled through the first half of the twentieth century. The story that follows is true.

I worked on this book in the time that I could wrest from my primary responsibility of working to build African Studies at the University of North Carolina at Chapel Hill (UNC). I completed much of the rewriting of my father's manuscript at the foot of Table Mountain in Cape Town, South Africa. I thank Julius Nyang'oro, my department chair, and Jim Leloudis, director of the Center for Undergraduate Excellence at UNC, for this opportunity. Due to the unusual nature of this project for an Africanist, it took no small amount of encouragement from key people to keep me involved in it. Theda Perdue and Mike Green never failed to prod me forward with their questions on my progress. Theda, who invited me to publish this book in her series, and three anonymous reviewers provided feedback that was essential during the later stages of assembling the final draft. Mike contributed to Theda's comments and provided critical corrections to errors in the original drafts, including corrections concerning obscure facts about automobiles of the era. Peggy Lambert sent me a copy of a document Sibbald Smith, my great-grandfather, wrote on the history of the family. I thank her for her generosity. I thank Gary Dunham, who is no longer with the University of Nebraska Press, but whose enthusiasm for the project convinced me to go with Nebraska, and Matthew Bokovoy and Elisabeth Chretien, who ably carried this project to completion.

To my father I extend my gratitude for devoting considerable effort toward putting these stories on paper, and to my mother gratitude for the patience to put up with his obsessions. My aunts and uncles I thank for sharing this experience with my father, even if they remember it differently. And it goes without saying that I thank my grandparents Leonard and Carrie Lambert, who raised their family at a remarkable time and whose hard work made all of this possible.

Most of all I thank my family. My wife, Valerie, chose to become part of this story and provided invaluable encouragement and constructive feedback at key times. She shared various drafts with her classes over the years and convinced me that there was a reason to move forward on the manuscript. Without her input this project would have never been completed. My daughters, Jessica and Hailey, did not choose to be part of this story, but their story is nonetheless told in these pages. You have and will make this book meaningful. I love the life I have with all of you.

I met Comanche cultural critic Paul Chaat Smith once, in a Durham bar. During our conversation I explained to him that some Eastern Cherokees opposed the casino on religious grounds. He asked if this was because of their adherence to traditional Indian beliefs. I said, "Good heavens no. It's because they are Baptists." Paul pondered this for a moment and asked, "When are we going to stop lying about Indian religion?" About a year later he published *Everything You Know about Indians Is Wrong,* and this convinced me that you could write about Indians as though they were just plain folks. The task he sets for us is to understand Indian experience not through the exotic and romantic, but through the everyday, or as he puts it, by looking at "the ground beneath our feet." I like to think that this memoir will in some way further the project he started.

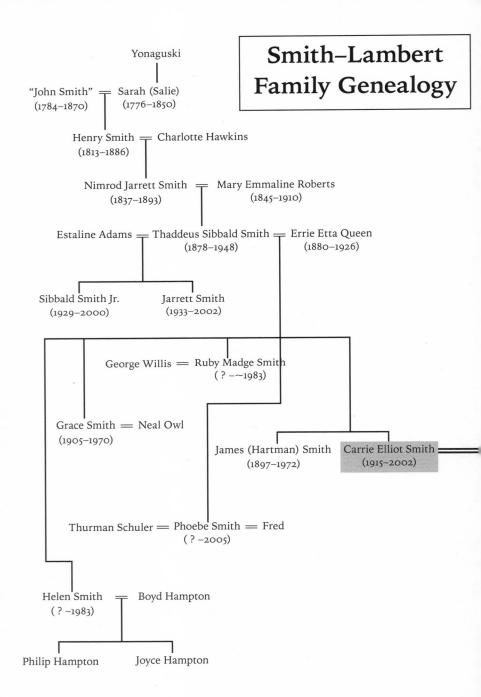

Yonaguski

"John Smith" ══ Sarah (Salie)
(1784–1870)   (1776–1850)

**Smith–Lambert
Family Genealogy**

Henry Smith ══ Charlotte Hawkins
(1813–1886)

Nimrod Jarrett Smith ══ Mary Emmaline Roberts
(1837–1893)   (1845–1910)

Estaline Adams ══ Thaddeus Sibbald Smith ══ Errie Etta Queen
                       (1878–1948)   (1880–1926)

Sibbald Smith Jr.   Jarrett Smith
(1929–2000)   (1933–2002)

George Willis ══ Ruby Madge Smith
                      (? –~1983)

Grace Smith ══ Neal Owl
(1905–1970)

James (Hartman) Smith   Carrie Elliot Smith ══
(1897–1972)   (1915–2002)

Thurman Schuler ══ Phoebe Smith ══ Fred
                          (? –2005)

Helen Smith ══ Boyd Hampton
(? –1983)

Philip Hampton   Joyce Hampton

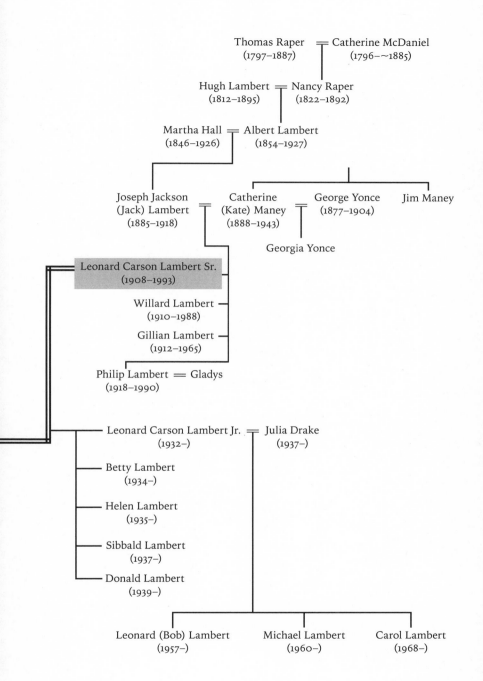

Thomas Raper
(1797–1887)

Catherine McDaniel
(1796–~1885)

Hugh Lambert
(1812–1895)

Nancy Raper
(1822–1892)

Martha Hall
(1846–1926)

Albert Lambert
(1854–1927)

Joseph Jackson
(Jack) Lambert
(1885–1918)

Catherine
(Kate) Maney
(1888–1943)

George Yonce
(1877–1904)

Jim Maney

Georgia Yonce

Leonard Carson Lambert Sr.
(1908–1993)

Willard Lambert
(1910–1988)

Gillian Lambert
(1912–1965)

Philip Lambert
(1918–1990)

Gladys

Leonard Carson Lambert Jr.
(1932–)

Julia Drake
(1937–)

Betty Lambert
(1934–)

Helen Lambert
(1935–)

Sibbald Lambert
(1937–)

Donald Lambert
(1939–)

Leonard (Bob) Lambert
(1957–)

Michael Lambert
(1960–)

Carol Lambert
(1968–)

Roots

My story begins in December 1931 when Mom and Dad got married. On that day they made their way down to the Sylva courthouse, a proud building that stands tall on a small hill in the middle of town. I really don't know how much honorable stuff went on up there on that hill, but it sure did stand there tall and proud. I would have to wait a long time before I would ever see a building as proud as that white courthouse was when it was standing tall against a clear blue sky. Not quite so grand was Bryson City's courthouse. That is where we went after Grandma Kate had been busted for selling moonshine. I remember talking to her through the bars in the window while Dad went in to bail her out. Courthouses are funny places. They always stand there so proud and majestic, but they host many not so proud events.

I think it was fitting that not just Mom and Dad but maybe some of my other relatives were married in that proud courthouse in Sylva. My family had a lot in common with it. You see, we were very proud of our family, especially the Smiths, Mom's family. It all went back to the fact that in the late 1800s my great-granddaddy, Nimrod Jarrett Smith, was, at that time, the most famous elected chief the Eastern Band of Cherokee Indians had ever had. There is no question that Chief Smith did some great things for the tribe. He built the school system, and he led the tribe through the perilous and formative post–Civil War years. Without him the Eastern Band of the Cherokee Indians, as a nation, might not even exist today.

But I also know that my great-grandpa Smith was a scoundrel. He was a heavy drinker and a womanizer, who by the time he died had fallen out of favor with his fellow tribal leaders, one of whom, James Blythe, was his own son-in-law. I have no doubt that hard living brought about his premature death in 1893 when he was only fifty-six. You can still see his tombstone up behind the grounds of the old Cherokee school in a small graveyard that seems out of place, surrounded as it is by a few scattered tribal administrative buildings. Buried next to him are a few of my other relatives—Jarrett's white wife, Mary, and a few of my ancestors from the other side of my family, my dad's great-grandfather Hugh Lambert and Nancy, his Cherokee wife.

My grandfather Sibbald Smith wrote a story about the history of the family that has since become part of family lore.[1] This story has it that Jarrett's white grandfather was involved in an Irish uprising and had to flee his native land.

Wanted by the British, he hid near the Irish coast under some corpses until nightfall, when a boat arrived to whisk him far away to American shores. On this side of the Atlantic the young man found himself in Charleston, where he came across some men who were heading to Georgia in search of gold. He decided to join these men, and he toiled in Habersham County in the Georgia highlands, looking for gold, but to no avail, so he continued deeper into the Cherokee Nation, where he eventually settled with some friendly Indians.

This man took to living as the Indians did. He farmed and hunted as they did, and he learned their language. He worked side-by-side with many Indians as though they were his own people and became close to a Cherokee chief named Yonaguski, with whose daughter he would fall in love. Her name was Salie. She was otherwise known as Sarah.

When he told the old chief that he wanted to marry his daughter, the chief gave the union his blessing, but on one condition. The chief told the young Irishman that although he had known him for some time, he still did not know his name and that if he wished to marry his daughter he would have to tell him who he was. The young Irishman thought for a while and decided that it was best that he not reveal his real identity lest word return to his British pursuers. He told the chief that he could call him "John Smith."

The old chief took ill and died during the winter following the marriage, and the young couple continued to live in the Georgia portion of the Cherokee Nation. It would not be long before the state of Georgia began to persecute the Indians, and they, like many other Indians, found it prudent at that point to move north across the border into North Carolina, where John Smith took a reservation in the name of himself and his wife on the Hiawassee River in the region of Fort Butler, what is today known as the city of Murphy.

John Smith's origins are shrouded in mystery. His grandsons even cast doubt on the story of his Irish origins when they claimed in their Guion-Miller applications that he was born in Culpepper, Virginia, instead of Ireland, as was claimed by my grandfather.[2] Nevertheless, Grandfather Sibbald's story has it that in the evenings he shared memories of his Irish homeland with his son Henry, even though he never shared with him his name, a secret that he would carry to his grave.

John Smith's grandson and Henry's son, Nimrod Jarrett Smith, was born in 1837, on Henry Smith's land at Longridge in the North Carolina Mountains of the Cherokee Nation on the eve of the Trail of Tears, the tragic removal of the Cherokee people to Indian Territory. We always referred to him as Jarrett, but he also had a Cherokee name, Tsa'la dihi. I have never quite nailed down all the facts as to why he and his family were spared the ordeal of the removal. I do know that the mountains of North Carolina were not like the fertile, flatter cotton-producing lands of Georgia, where, in the 1830s, most of the Cherokee Nation lived. As a group the whites of North Carolina probably did not much care who was living in the mountains at the western end of the state and never pushed the U.S. government to complete the job and send all the Indians to the West. I doubt that it would have been easy for the government to complete this job anyway, given the rugged mountainous terrain that characterizes the far western portion of the state.

The Cherokees knew this, and some of the Cherokees who lived in Georgia sought refuge in the North Carolina Mountains, an act that that made some Cherokees in North Carolina nervous, particularly the Qualla Indians, who lived north of the Cherokee Nation, along the banks of the Oconaluftee and Tuckasegee rivers. This is the band that lived in what is today known as the Qualla Boundary, or the primary track of land that comprises the main reservation of the Eastern Band of Cherokees. This is a fifty thousand–acre reservation in mountainous terrain. The major settlements are clustered along the flat lands that line the rivers that run through the valleys. The most important of these rivers are the Oconaluftee River, which flows down from the Smoky Mountains past Yellow Hill and through Birdtown; the Raven Fork, which also runs from the Smoky Mountains through Big Cove to the Oconaluftee River; and Soco Creek, which runs down from Soco Gap toward Cherokee.

This small band of Cherokees feared that they too would be subject to the removal if the U.S. government believed that they were offering refuge to the Georgia Indians. With the assistance of Will Thomas, the white businessman who came to be known as the white chief of the Cherokees, they successfully argued that they had renounced their citizenship in the Cherokee Nation following the treaty of 1819 and that because they were no longer Cherokee citizens, they were not subject to the conditions of the removal treaty.[3] According to Eastern Band legend their right to remain in North Carolina was sealed when the Qualla Indians brought Tsali and his family, a fugitive band of Cherokees, to justice on behalf of the government. The story has it that as Tsali and his family were being marched to a holding camp in preparation for their removal to Indian Territory, an altercation erupted between Tsali and his family's military escorts. Tsali killed one of the soldiers, and he and his family fled into the mountains, where they successfully eluded capture. General Winfield Scott, who was enforcing the Cherokee removal, agreed to let the other Cherokees who had not yet been removed remain in North Carolina if the Qualla Indians would bring Tsali to justice. Legend has it that when Tsali heard of this deal, he surrendered himself, sealing his status as a martyr. He and three others would be executed. Other more scholarly examinations of this episode paint a much less heroic picture. In these accounts Tsali flees and is tracked down and killed by his Cherokee brethren.[4]

My ancestors were not among the Qualla Indians at the time of the removal. They were living further south, near the present-day town of Murphy. The 1835 removal treaty included a clause that allowed those Cherokees who were deemed competent in the ways of the whites to remain in the east, but only after they had surrendered their property. At the outset of the removal the government started making a list of Indians who would be eligible to remain in North Carolina. Among the team compiling the list of Cherokees who wished to remain was a man named Nimrod S. Jarrett, who was surely my great-grandpa's namesake. Given that my great-grandpa Nimrod Jarrett Smith was born in 1837, one wonders if his father, Henry, bestowed this name on him because Nimrod Jarrett made it possible for Henry and his family to remain in North Carolina. To bolster Henry's chances of avoiding the removal, John Timpson, a contemporary and associate of Henry Smith, was on the team that decided who was "qualified" to remain.[5] Quite possibly, Henry and his family were spared the ordeal of the removal through the strength of their ties to these individuals. This is not to say Henry was not an able man in his own right, who deserved to be considered as competent as any white man. In the years following the removal he proved this by establishing himself as one of the wealthiest men in southwestern North Carolina, despite having been dispossessed of much of his property during the removal.

While Jarrett's mother, Charlotte, spoke only Cherokee, his father, Henry, had received an education in English. He was much better educated than his illiterate Irish father, and he made very good use of his education. He very likely studied at the Valley Town Baptist Mission that was led by Reverend Evan Jones, the missionary who would follow the Cherokees to Indian Territory.[6] He might have also worked there as a translator, a job that I believe he also did for the government officials who compiled the pre-removal census of the Cherokees. Following the removal Henry used his skills to represent Indians who had remained in North Carolina and who were making claims against the government. He made many of these claims on the part of Cherokees who were attempting to claim property that was taken from them during the removal.

Knowing the value of an education, Henry made sure that his son Jarrett would receive the same privileges of education he had enjoyed. I'm sure that Jarrett's education, combined with his commanding presence, was among the assets that would eventually make him a leader of the Eastern Cherokees.

Nimrod Jarrett Smith was still a young man when the Civil War broke out, and at age twenty-five he enlisted in the Sixty-ninth North Carolina Infantry as a first sergeant of Company B. This company was part of the legion of Cherokee soldiers that Will Thomas, the famous "white chief" of the Eastern Cherokees, had organized. Thomas was under the mistaken impression that the South would win the war, so he aligned the legion with the Confederate Army.

The legion made their way to Knoxville, their new base, where according to John Finger, historian of the Eastern Cherokee, the Indians became an attraction, drawing people in to see them dance and entertain.[7] It is probably a good thing that, for the most part, they managed to sit out the war in this way. As Finger points out, the Thomas Legion was poorly trained for battle and, to be honest, was prob-

ably in no mood to fight anyway.[8] Many eventually tired of
the war, left Knoxville, and returned to their homes. As for
Great-Grandpa Smith, he stayed with the legion until the
end of the war in 1865 but served without distinction. Then
he returned to the western North Carolina Mountains and
became active in tribal politics. By then Will Thomas had
begun to lose his mind and was in no shape to continue
to lead this small band of Cherokees. As the Indians began to take over their own affairs, Jarrett was right in the
thick of things. In 1868 Jarrett served as clerk of the council
that drafted the first Eastern Cherokee Tribal Constitution.

In 1880, following the death of Lloyd Welch, the first
elected chief of the Eastern Cherokees, Nimrod Jarrett was
appointed to fill Chief Welch's unexpired term. He would
manage to get himself reelected twice, and he remained in
office until the end of 1891—eleven years. No other elected
chief of the Eastern Band of Cherokee Indians has ever
served a longer uninterrupted term.

During his tenure as principal chief Great-Grandpa Smith
accomplished much for our family to be proud of. He secured the right of the Eastern Cherokees to their land in
North Carolina and began to build schools on the reservation. For several years he spent much of his time dealing
with a lawsuit the tribe had filed against the Western Cherokees over the right of the Eastern Cherokees to money al-
located for the removal under the 1835 treaty. And perhaps
most important, in 1889 he incorporated the Eastern Band
under North Carolina state law, an act that would have long-
term implications by insuring that the tribe would be able to

protect their land as a corporate asset in the face of federal efforts in the 1890s to allot the land of the Eastern Band.[9]

I would imagine that for the most part Great-Grandpa Smith was diligent in his duties. Although the chief was entitled to an annual salary of five hundred dollars, I believe that he never received any of his salary because the tribe was so poor.

As Finger documents, in the later years of his political career he became embroiled in many arguments with the tribal council, and his popularity began to wane.[10] To make matters worse, Great-Grandpa Smith was not blessed by the strongest of moral backbones, and he was prone to moral lapses. His fellow tribal members accused him of drunkenness, assault, and even prostituting one of his daughters to a local storekeeper. By all accounts Great-Grandpa Smith was tall and handsome, attributes that he did not hesitate to use to his advantage. As my family remembers it, Jarrett often left his family to provide for themselves as he traveled to Washington, tending to tribal business. I am sure that many women fell victim to his good looks and outgoing personality during his travels and found themselves counted among the many affairs to which Jarrett was a party. One of these affairs reportedly tore a Cherokee family apart. I feel sorry for his white wife, Mary Emmaline Roberts Smith, who had to endure his philandering and raise his children alone.

His reputation was so tarnished by the end of his tenure as chief that, according to Finger, the U.S. government sent an agent to Cherokee to investigate his conduct.[11] After the agent presented his findings to the War Department, it informed the tribe that if Chief Smith were reelected for yet another term, the government would not allow him to take office. I guess that the government agent had reason to believe the claims made by some tribal members that he had tried to enrich himself at the expense of his people. Nevertheless, he failed miserably at that, and he died in 1893, well before his time, a broken, poor man who was at odds with his own people.

Grandpa Smith, Thaddeus Sibbald Smith, was born in 1878 and had the unenviable task of living in the long shadow cast by his father. Although Sibbald probably had a distant relationship with his father because Nimrod Jarrett spent so much time traveling, there is no question that he was acquainted with both his father's accomplishments and his moral failings. Sadly, Grandpa Smith modeled himself more after the latter than the former.

He inherited his father's good looks, and like his father he was well educated. He spent some time studying at the Carlisle Indian Industrial School in Pennsylvania, although he apparently did not think much of the school. When he tried to leave after his first year, Richard Pratt, the school's founder and a renowned Indian educator, the man who made famous the phrase "kill the Indian and save the man," said that Sibbald would have to work off a debt before he would be allowed to return home. Sibbald's mother, Mary Smith, had to implore the ethnologist James Mooney to intervene to secure his release.[12] When he finished his studies, Sibbald embarked on a career as a surveyor. Like his father's his work required that he travel for long stretches of time.

Between jobs, like his father, he fought for Indian causes. John Finger describes how he helped secure the right of Eastern Cherokees to vote in local elections and, with others, helped clarify the confusing legal status of the North Carolina Cherokees. On top of all this he was also a special agent entrusted with ferreting out whiskey stills, a job he probably accepted so that he could collect bribes.[13] At any rate I am sure that he failed miserably at this, as most conscientious Prohibition officers were shot dead early in their careers. Grandpa Smith managed to live to the age of seventy, when prostate cancer finally killed him.

He had ten children with his first wife, Errie, and then she died in 1926. Soon after that Grandpa started courting again, even though I would suspect that he was seeing other women even when Errie was alive. For a while he even courted my dad's mother, Grandma Lambert, and this is who many of his children, including my mom, wanted him to marry. However, this was not to be. Instead Grandpa found his second wife, Estaline Adams, during one of his many visits to Cherokee County, in the far southwest corner of the state.

Estaline was a mere girl when she married my grandfather. She would bear him eight more children, and sadly, she had to raise these children in poverty. You see, in the time I knew him Grandpa never appeared to have a regular job. Nor did he seem to want one. It seemed that he spent all his time talking about Indian problems and complaining that the government was doing nothing about them. By then poor old Grandpa's influence on Cherokee policy had withered away. It did not help that by then the tribe had a very popular, progressive chief named Jarrett Blythe. I am sure that the fact that Chief Blythe was Grandpa's first cousin burned Grandpa up more than anything. I am sure that he thought that it was he who should have been chief, just like his father.

By the time I came to know Grandpa Smith, he was just a shell of a man. He was truly a man without purpose. Nor was Grandpa Smith pleasant to be around, so I stayed away from him, not that he would have wanted me around anyway. I can't remember once that he ever spoke to me. He had no patience for children, including his own. I guess this explains why he was never around to care for his first family. Even though he was at home to raise his second family, it seemed that he still didn't take very good care of them.

Instead of working, Grandpa spent most of his time sitting at home gazing out the window. Mom claimed that Grandpa Smith had to stay home because he was afraid to let his child-bride out of sight. Mom said that he was afraid she would take up with another man. I would not have been surprised if this happened on occasion. I remember some Sunday afternoons when Estaline and my aunt Phoebe would talk and giggle about some taxi driver in Bryson City. Estaline also told stories about how the principal at Birdtown Day School would drive her to Bryson City and how he would let his hand slip off the gear shift and rest on her leg. Later, when I ran the Birdtown shop in the early 1950s, I would see Estaline walking past my gift shop in the morning on her way to work at Curly Lambert's motel on Soco Road. It seemed that she was always very happy. Mom said she was so happy because she and Curly were carrying on. But I don't know if I should trust what Mom said about Estaline; Mom made it no secret that she hated her, and to be honest, Mom probably had good reason to feel this way. After all, Estaline did make it clear that she wanted little to do with Grandpa's first family.

I guess Mom never forgave her dad for marrying Estaline. After they married, life became very hard for Mom. But Mom's list of reasons for being angry with Grandpa did not start there. Grandpa's first family was even poorer than Grandpa's second family. Grandpa was almost never at home while his first wife, Errie, was still alive. She was solely responsible for looking after the children, caring for the crops, and tending to the farm animals. Their economic situation was sad indeed. He was so neglectful of his family that his daughter Phoebe was six months old before he made time to see her. To make matters worse, death arrived often on their doorstep, and Mom watched as, one by one, her siblings died.

Mom was only eleven when her mother died. After Errie died, Grandpa immediately started looking for places to send his children—places for them to work or to study. He farmed the children out to whoever would take them. Grandpa sent Mom, Helen, and a couple of her other sisters to Misenheimer, near Charlotte, to attend Mitchell

Home School, a girls' boarding school. I am sure the Indian Agency probably covered the expenses; there is no other way Grandpa Smith could have afforded it. Over the years the government sent many Indian children to white boarding schools in an attempt to rid the children of their Indian ways. I do not know how long Mom and her sisters stayed at the Mitchell Home School, but according to my mom, all three of them hated the school.

They returned to Cherokee when Mom was about thirteen. But it was not long before Grandpa had them on the road again, this time to Mars Hill College, where they worked as live-in maids to the Elliott family, old friends of Grandpa and the inspiration for Mom's middle name. While they were there, Mom took a liking to Boyd Hampton, a white farm boy who lived between Mars Hill and Marshall. Later Boyd would take Helen as his wife. This seeded bad feelings between Mom and her sister Helen that would last the rest of their lives. After staying in Mars Hill a while, Mom and her sister Helen returned to Cherokee.

The matriarch on Dad's side of the family was my grandma Kate Maney Lambert. She was born in 1888 and lived until late July 1943, when a bad case of tuberculosis killed her. Grandma Lambert was a white woman, even though she probably did have a trace of Cherokee blood. Being white or Indian was not simply a question of ancestry, as it seems to have become for many today. If your name was not on the Baker Roll of the Eastern Band, you weren't a member of the tribe, and you weren't an Indian. In spite of this

Grandma lived almost all of her life on the reservation, and she even owned reservation land after her husband Jack died. What I remember most about Kate is that she had one of the nicest homes in Cherokee. It was down in Bird-town across the road from the Oconaluftee River, which wound its way along the mountain bottom.

This is not to say that Grandma Lambert always had a nice home. In fact I think it would be fair to say that she lived a hard life—most of it in poverty. Her life was so hard that she lived to see two husbands into the ground. Her first husband, George Yonce, died in 1904 in a logging train accident in Marion. Soon after George's death Grandma married his first cousin and my grandpa Jack Lambert.

Grandpa Jack was an Indian. His grandpa was Hugh Lambert, the white man buried up in Cherokee next to the grave of Great-Grandpa Smith. It is said that in the 1830s Hugh's brother volunteered to help round up the Cherokees for the removal. When he returned home, he told Hugh of the beauty of the territory the Cherokees were being forced to leave behind, thus inspiring Hugh to head for the southwest corner of the state. Early in his journey Hugh lodged in the home of Thomas Raper, a white man who had married into the Cherokee Nation. Hugh fell in love with and married Thomas's daughter Nancy. Almost all the Lamberts in the Eastern Band trace their ancestry back to this union.

I never knew Grandpa Jack. He was whisked away at the tender age of thirty-three by the great flu epidemic of 1918. This meant that he was gone before the Baker Roll had been assembled. This was the roll that was assembled in 1924 in preparation for the dissolution of the tribe.[14] Had he lived, he would have been listed as having just a trace of Indian blood. Some of his fellow Eastern Cherokees even thought that he and his children should not be included on the roll. What I do know is that what Indian blood he had came straight out of the family of Moytoy of Tellico, the Cherokee chief who was proclaimed emperor of all the Cherokees in 1730 by the self-appointed British envoy Alexander Cumming.[15] This meant that he was related to pretty much everyone who was anyone in the old Cherokee Nation that once thrived in north Georgia before Andrew Jackson sent the Cherokees to Indian Territory.

Poor old Grandma. By the time she was thirty-eight she had already been twice widowed. To make matters worse, when Jack died, he didn't leave Kate with much except for a brood of six children to tend: Leonard, Willard, Lula, Leona, Gillian, and Philip.

My dad, Leonard Senior, told me that his pa, Jack, always worked hard but never could provide for his family. They were always very poor—even poorer than Grandpa Smith's family. The few jobs that Grandpa Jack was able to obtain didn't pay much, which I can understand. Times were hard in the mountains, and jobs were scarce. But Grandpa Jack was also a real dreamer, and he spent most of his life chasing rainbows. Dad said that Grandpa Jack lived as though his fortune lay just beyond the next hill, down in the next valley. He kept chasing those rainbows and dragging his family from here to there as he chased after his dreams.

He might have been chasing rainbows, but he never found one; he just moved from one wretched job to the next. My dad told me that when he was young, Grandpa moved the family at least four times a year. According to Dad once he even moved the family twice in one day. Jack usually kept his family on or near the reservation, but at least once he moved them all the way to South Carolina in search of riches. Nevertheless, I guess moving so much wasn't as much trouble as it sounds. The family did not own much. I doubt that Jack's family ever lived in a house bigger than a one- or two-bedroom shack. When they moved, all Jack needed was an oxen-drawn sled to haul a stove, a few clothes, a couple of beds, and some pots and pans.

One time Jack moved the family up into a steep hollow off the road to Birdtown, about a mile from Cherokee. They had two shacks—one serving as a kitchen and the other as a bedroom. One day Dad and his father went up the hollow from the shacks to cut a tree for firewood. Jack chose a large slender pine tree. He cut the tree and let it fall parallel to the hollow. The tree fell with the top pointing down the steep hollow, and just as it hit the ground, it started sliding down the hollow, straight for the shack that served as their kitchen. The tree picked up speed at a frightening rate and hit the kitchen head-on. It went straight through the kitchen and came to a stop with the top half of the tree extruding from the lower wall of the kitchen. Grandma and a couple of kids were in the kitchen, but luckily, the tree missed them.

Dad said Grandpa Jack was a part-time preacher, but I know that he was never employed by a church full-time. Dad said Jack loved to sing, and he was always holding family singing sessions. Once Dad even tried to get us to do a little family singing, perhaps because he had fond memories of singing with his family as a child, but we had miserable voices.

After Jack died, Grandma did what she had to do to feed her children. Once she moved all the way to Florida to do some work. I do not know what took her so far away, but I suppose that she must have been up to no good. At least that was the impression that I got from my mom. Many years later Mom raised a ruckus when her son Don decided to move there. Mom was convinced that Florida was an evil place.

I guess Mom might have been right to think that Grandma was up to no good in Florida. I know it could have been true, since I know that Grandma meddled in some shady business on the reservation. In the 1920s she started selling moonshine, and maybe she was doing some other illegal things. Back in the 1920s and early 1930s there were not many tourists coming to the reservation, so Grandma sold most of her moonshine to Indians and white timber cutters.

The Indians and the whites liked moonshine, and Grandma did pretty well. Before long she had saved enough money to buy a little twenty-acre farm in Birdtown on the main road between Bryson City and Cherokee. As a timber company railroad ran right in front of her house, it would have been hard for her to find a better place to run her bootlegging business.

In the 1920s logging was a big industry in the mountains, and the timber companies used the railroad to haul timber out of the mountains. After a hard day at work the timber workers had little to do on the reservation, except drink. It was too bad for them that it was illegal to sell alcohol on the reservation, but not for everyone else.

Mountain people say they do not like drinking. They say that drinking is against the Bible's teachings. But don't believe it, they like alcohol, they just don't like legal alcohol. In almost every family in Cherokee someone made a living by selling or making moonshine. The police didn't do much about it because the bootleggers paid them off. The preachers were also happy because when the bootleggers had cash, the collection plates would be brimming with money. The preachers knew this, so they always preached on the evils of liquor. Religion was as good a reason as any to keep legal whiskey out of the mountains and off the reservation. Grandma made good on this arrangement, and it wasn't long before she had money to buy an additional fifteen acres in a cove across the river.

Some people might have a problem with this, but I don't blame Grandma for bootlegging. Life was hard for a poor widow who did not have a regular job or her husband's pension check to live on. With bootlegging all she had to do was sit on her front porch, and the moonshine sold itself. When I was a boy, I used to pass her house going to and from school. Each day I would see her sitting on the porch.

I would always cross the road and spend a little time talking with Grandma before continuing on my way across the river and up to the cove where we lived. I'm sure Grandma wasn't waiting on the porch to see me. She was sitting there waiting for her next customer.

My dad was just ten when Grandpa Jack died. After Grandpa died, my dad went to the boarding school in Cherokee, where he stayed until the ninth grade. After he quit school, he and his brother Willard went down the Little Tennessee River to where the Aluminum Company of American (ALCOA) was building the Cheoah Dam and powerhouse, and they landed jobs as muleskinners. They led a team of mules that was used to power construction equipment at the project. Dad and Willard were good at this job. They had been working with animals all their lives.

After Dad and Willard worked at this job for a while, they heard of higher-paying jobs down in Alabama. So they quit their ALCOA jobs and headed for Alabama, riding freight trains as hoboes. When they arrived in Alabama, they discovered that the rumor that there were good jobs to be had was nothing but malarkey. All they could find was low-paying work on a farm in a black work gang. This did not please the blacks, who did not want to see two Indians taking jobs that could be filled by local unemployed blacks. Dad and Willard were threatened to the point that they feared for their lives, so they quit this job.

They quickly learned that farmwork was the only work they could find, and their money soon ran out. A kindly black couple took pity on them and put them up for a few days. Then they were back on the road looking for work. Eventually, a sheriff picked them up and threatened to throw them in jail if they did not find their way out of the county. Afraid that the sheriff would make good on his threat, they jumped on the next freight train and headed back to Cherokee.

Willard left the reservation one more time. For a while he and his first wife, or maybe just a woman friend, lived near Gastonia, where he worked in a textile mill. But Grandma Kate wanted all her children to be nearby, so she went all the way to Gastonia and brought her boy home. Willard left his woman and child behind in Gastonia. Later Willard married Ethel Murphy and spent the rest of his life on the reservation working as a night watchman or laborer.

Dad also left Cherokee again in search of work. This time he and a friend went to a farming area near Philadelphia in search of work. It didn't take long for Dad's friend to become homesick and return to Cherokee. Dad, however, stayed and landed a job on a dairy farm. The job was demanding. He had to milk about twenty-five cows twice a day, seven days a week. This meant that he never got a day off, something he was not happy about. He worked there until he was offered a job on a crop farm that had just a couple of cows to milk. This gave Dad part of each weekend free. He did well, and soon he had enough money to buy a used car and some new clothes. Before long he had found himself a Pennsylvania sweetheart to keep him company.

But Dad's good life in the Pennsylvania farmlands did not last. Grandma wanted him to come home. She told her daughter Leona to send him a letter telling Dad that his mother was on her deathbed and that Dad had to come back to Cherokee to see her one more time. Dad quit his job, kissed his sweetheart goodbye, and boarded the next train for North Carolina.

A couple of days later, when he got off the train at Grandma's house, no one was at home to greet him. Dad waited on the porch until that afternoon, when the train from Bryson City arrived, and Grandma, Leona, and Willard got off. Then Dad knew that he had been had. If it were me, I would have packed my bags and headed straight back to Pennsylvania. But not Dad. He never returned to the North, nor did he say much of his days there. He probably knew better than to do that because Mom was fiercely jealous of Dad's old sweetheart.

The Cove

After Mom and Dad married, they had nothing and nowhere to live. Their only option was to move in with Grandma Lambert on her small farm in Birdtown. Her house was nice. It had a porch, salon, kitchen, cellar, small attic, and three small bedrooms. The farm had a small barn and a two-seat outhouse that straddled a small creek that emptied into the Oconaluftee River. Grandma did not have electricity, so she used a wood-burning stove for heat and cooking and oil lamps for light. What made her house stand out from others on the reservation is that it had a pipe that ran water from a nearby spring into her kitchen sink.

Even though the house was nice, it was far too small for the small army—Grandma, Willard, Gillian, and Philip—that was already living there. It did not help that this was the home of Dad's mom, which meant that Dad remained more of a mama's boy than a husband. Despite the fact that the house was overcrowded, I am sure that Grandma was happy about the arrangement. All her boys were under her nose, and she had her daughter-in-law to boss around. Needless to say, Mom was not happy about the situation. There she was, sixteen, pregnant, and living with her mother-in-law. She has told me that she did all the housework, and I am sure that Mom was not shy about letting everyone know how miserable she was in that house. Poor Dad, he probably caught an earful every evening when he came home from work.

I guess one good thing that could be said about the situation was that Dad did work. In fact he was the only man in that house to have steady work. He did not have good jobs; he just took whatever he could find. At one time or another he worked as farm hand, laborer, timber cutter, and just about any other manual job that you can imagine.

During the 1930s Dad's work situation would begin to improve. Until then the roads in Cherokee—if you can call them that—were, at best, little more than trails plied by horse- and oxen-drawn sleds. Just a few of the better trails could handle a wheeled wagon. Even a major route such as the main road from Cherokee to Bryson City, the road that ran in front of Grandma's house, was just a dirt road. In the 1930s the government began to pave roads throughout the mountains. At the same time the Indian Agency began a project to build roads to all communities on the reservation. Dad could always find work on these roads, and this was good work. Work that paid cash. The farmers Dad had worked for paid in produce—a gallon of molasses, a jar of honey, a bag of corn, or some farm animal.

Dad did fairly well with this roadwork. Before long he managed to have a few head of livestock running on Grandma's place. This turned out to be a very good thing for Mom. Mom had been pushed to the limit by the situation in Grandma Lambert's house, and she convinced Dad to trade a few head of livestock for Grandma's fifteen-acre cove on the other side of the river.

As soon as he had secured the land, Dad started building a small one-room log cabin in the cove. But progress was slow. Dad was working on the roads and had little time to devote to building our home. Eventually, Grandma Kate's brother, Jim Maney, stepped in and forced Philip and Gillian get off their lazy asses and help Dad complete the work. Once the log cabin had been raised, Mom, Dad, and I moved in. It was very modest. It was no bigger than a one-car garage. This is where we would live until Dad finished the main house.

We moved to the cove with Dad's team of steers, a cow, a pig, a few chickens, a sled, a plow, some gardening hand tools, an ax, a saw, and an awl. Dad furnished the cabin with a wood-burning cook stove, a steel-frame bed, a homemade wood-plank table, and a couple of homemade chairs. We used a big cotton bag filled with straw for a mattress. Our water came from a spring, but we never did have an outhouse. Instead we relieved ourselves in the woods, which, I can assure you, is not easy when it is cold and rainy.

Dad finished the main house shortly after we moved to the cove. With a kitchen, dining room, bedroom, and front room, this house was much larger than the single-room log cabin we had been living in. A porch ran along the front and one side of the house. The walls were made of thin single vertical eight-inch boards. Dad used one-inch slats to cover the cracks and then covered the inside walls with heavy-grade brown paper for insulation. The ceiling was made out of tongue-and-groove wood planks. Our woodstove sent heat straight up and out of the house through the ceiling cracks. It was a good house. But it was also a cold house, and particularly so during the long cold mountain winters.

Dad kept two cows, and each spring they calved. Our cows also gave us about four gallons of milk each day. This was more than enough for us to have some to drink and to make butter. During the summer Mom stored the milk and butter in the spring to keep them fresh. We had twenty-five free-range hens that laid more eggs than we needed. About once a week Dad took a big bucket of eggs to the store and swapped them for flour, sugar, salt, spices, and meat.

The best thing about having chickens was that once a month a hen or rooster would find its way to our Sunday dinner table. Mom would catch the chicken, and then she would either cut the chicken's head off with an ax, or she would hold the chicken's head and twirl the chicken around and around until its neck snapped. Then she would leave the chicken to flop around under a bushel basket. Mom dipped the dead chicken in hot water to loosen its feathers. This hot-water bath made it much easier for her to pluck the feathers, which she would use to stuff our pillows. Once the hot water bath was complete, Mom singed the chicken with burning paper to remove the remaining down.

The cove was very fertile, and we could almost support ourselves solely off of what we grew. Each year Mom and Dad cleared away trees at the edge of our existing fields. This virgin soil was extremely rich and grew wonderful crops, so good that we never had to use commercial fertilizer. Cow and chicken manure were more than good enough. We raised corn, onions, white potatoes, sweet potatoes, cabbage, carrots, beets, lettuce, beans, pumpkins, squash, cucumbers, radishes, peas, turnips, mustard greens, hot peppers, and bell peppers. We had an apple orchard of twelve trees, blueberries, blackberries, strawberries, greens, walnuts, persimmons, and grapes. The only food we had to buy was lard, flour, sugar, oatmeal, salt, spices, and now and then a beef roast.

During the autumn a sorghum maker would set up his equipment in the area. Farmers in the area would bring their cane to him so that he could process it into syrup. Usually we did not grow sorghum, but one year we did. That year the sorghum maker set up his equipment at our end of the swinging bridge that crossed the Oconaluftee River. It was just on the other side of the Coopers' house.

We kids really enjoyed watching this cane made into syrup. We were really fascinated by the process, and I can still remember how it was done. It was really simple. All he had were a rotary cane press and a cooking vat. He used an ox to pull a long lever in circles to turn the press. One of his assistants fed the cane stalks into the press, and the juice from the pressed stalks flowed into a bucket.

The syrup itself was made in a large copper boiling vat that was perched atop a two-foot-high dirt firing chamber. The syrup maker lit a fire in the chamber under the vat at the end where the syrup discharged and pushed the fire up that length of the vat. This allowed the smoke and heat to travel under the vat and up a small flue located at the end, where he poured juice into the vat. The boiling vat had baffles about every eight inches. This lengthened the time the juices were over the firing chamber. As the juice flowed over the hot chamber, the water evaporated, leaving behind sweet syrup. When the juices had completed their passage over the firing chamber, they flowed as syrup out of a drain spout into a bucket.

Dad hauled several loads of sorghum on our ox sled to make syrup. The fire was lit in late afternoon, and the syrup making began in the early evening. Several hours later it was over. We kids had a great time, playing and tasting the syrup. Mom and Dad enjoyed seeing their friends who were also making syrup. None of us had much money, so Dad, like most people, let the syrup maker keep 10 percent of our syrup.

We always grew several kinds of vegetables in the same field at the same time. Beans and pumpkins were planted alongside corn. This way the corn supported the bean vines. In the autumn we gathered the ears of corn, shucked them, and then stored the ears in the corncrib. We stored the shucks, which we fed to our cows, in the barn loft. We cut the corn stalks and stored them in vertical bundles in the fields until we used them as winter feed for our cows. The corn kernels were either fed to chickens or ground into cornmeal. Mom used the meal to make cornbread or cornmeal mush, one of our breakfast foods.

We almost never had to buy cornmeal. Dad would take our corn to the water-powered gristmill to be ground into meal. Water-powered mills are ideal for grinding grain, as there are no fuel fumes to taint the meal. We usually took about a bushel of corn each time, and the miller would take about 15 percent of the cornmeal as payment.

In the summer, during cool mornings and after lunch in the early afternoons, we picked wild strawberries, huckleberries, blackberries, and raspberries. Mom used these berries to make jams and jellies. We also sold wild blackberries to the Birdtown School for fifteen cents a gallon. The school cooks would use the berries to make jellies and jams for the students. In the autumn we gathered black and white walnuts, grapes, and persimmons.

Dad built an apple bin in the bedroom. The bedroom never got too warm, nor did it get too cold, so it was an ideal place to store apples during the winter. We buried our potatoes and cabbage in the fields. Dad would dig a hole about four feet square and about six inches deep. He covered the bottom of the hole with straw and placed the potatoes and cabbage heads on the straw and then covered them with a thick layer of straw. Then he placed about six inches of dirt on top of the straw. This protected the vegetables from freezing. When Mom needed potatoes or cabbage, she cleared some dirt away and removed the vegetables she needed, and then she replaced the dirt. Mom stored onions in our barn, tied in bunches that hung from the rafters.

Mom always worked hard catering to us children. However, she worked harder than ever during the summer and fall, so Dad and we children tried to help her whenever we could. Mom canned beans, greens, carrots, beets, squash, corn, peas, and vegetable soup. Mom had to make sure that the jars were free of bacteria and air when the jars were sealed. She filled the clean jars with the cooked food and then heated the food to a temperature that, with any luck, would kill all the bacteria. She sealed the jars while they were still steaming. This prevented any air from remaining in the jar. Mom rarely failed to do this right, but now and then a little air would remain in the jar, and the food would spoil.

In the 1930s the Indian Agency provided everyone with access to a pressure cooker. Now Mom wouldn't have to place the jar in boiling water. Instead she placed the jars in the cooker with water about halfway up the jars. Then she sealed the cooker and increased the temperature until the pressure in the cooker was quite high. When Mom opened the cooker the jar lids fastened tight. The superheating removed any air and killed the bacteria. This might have been sanitary, but it was still dangerous. Now and then we would hear of a cooker exploding.

Mom pickled green beans, chow-chow, kraut, and corn on the cob. She packed the raw vegetables tightly into two- or three-gallon "stone jars." The jars were not really stone. Rather they were just a very hard pottery that the mountain people called stone. After she filled the jars with the vegetables, she poured in salt brine. She then placed a weight on the jar lids and placed the jars in a cool dark place. Before long the pickled vegetables would be ready to eat. Mom's pickled vegetables were the best I have ever eaten. The kraut always had the core of the cabbage head and a hint of hot peppers.

Mom made dried apples, bleached apples, and dried green beans. She made the latter, which we called leather britches, by stringing green beans on a thread with a needle and then hanging them in the sun to dry. She made dried apples by slicing the apples and then placing the slices in the sun to dry. She bleached the apple slices with sulfur smoke.

Mom also made pickles with vinegar, always following the "signs" from the *Farmer's Almanac*. She said that kraut made when the signs were in the feet stage would taste like dirty feet.[1] In fact, whether we were planting seeds or preserving food, we did so in accordance with the astrological signs.

Next to the Cherokee Fair hog-killing time was my favorite time of the year. Each spring Mom and Dad purchased a small piglet and fed the pig very well with table scraps and corn. By November the small pig would have grown into a large two-hundred-pound hog.

On a cold day in late November Dad would build a roaring fire under an iron pot filled with water—the same pot that Mom used to wash our clothes. Then Dad would set up an eight-foot tripod made from sapling poles on which to hang the dead hog. The tripod was tied at the peak with a rope. Nearby he placed a few planks on the ground on which to lay the hog while he removed its hair. When the water was near boiling, Dad led the hog from the pen to this killing area.

Dad killed the hog by hitting it on the forehead with a five-pound sledgehammer. Sometimes one whack was not enough, and Dad would have to take another whack at the hog to finish it off. Later on, when we were living in Tennessee and Mars Hill, Dad would shoot our hogs in the head with a 22-caliber gun. Sometimes it took more than one bullet.

Once the hog had flopped to the ground, Dad would stick a butcher knife into the hog's heart and drain its blood onto the ground. After the blood had drained and the mess was cleaned up, Dad covered the hog with burlap sacks. Then he poured boiling water on the sacks and let the hog soak for a few minutes. This made the hair easier to scrape off, which Dad and Mom did with a sharp butcher knife. It was just like shaving with a straight razor. This work took about an hour. With the hair removed, Dad would cut a small hole in each hind leg and then stick the sharpened end of a short tree limb through these holes. Dad then used a pulley at the top of the tripod to hoist the hog up such that it would be hanging upside-down. Now Dad was ready for the real butchering to begin. He started by cutting off the head. Then he cut the belly from stern to starboard and let the entrails and organs fall into a tub. Then Dad would move the tub to the side so that Mom could begin her work.

Mom removed the liver and took it to the kitchen. Then she returned to cut the fat from the guts. It took quite a while for Mom to trim the fat. She removed all the fat from the entrails and all the other pig parts and put the pieces of fat in the big iron pot. The fat was heated and rendered of the liquid fat that Mom and Dad stored in empty coffee cans. The remaining cracklings in the pot were removed from the tub and saved to be used in cornbread.

While Mom was working, Dad cut the two shoulders from the hog and then removed the two pieces of belly meat. This left just the hams and backbone hanging from the tripod. The backbone held the loin, which I thought was the tastiest part of the hog. Dad cut the backbone and the loins from the hams. Dad cured the hams, at least one shoulder, and one side of belly meat. He placed the meat on a table in the garage and poured about half an inch of salt on the meat. It didn't take long for the salt to cure and preserve the meat.

Mom cooked the head and used it to make souse meat. Mom fried some of the liver, and with the remainder she made liver mush. Mom and Dad usually ground a piece of side meat and a shoulder for sausage. They seasoned the ground meat with sage, hot dried peppers, black pepper, and salt. Then they formed the meat into patties, which they fried and canned in hot liquid fat in quart or half-gallon mason jars. The first few meals after the hog killing were real feasts. For these meals Mom cooked the backbone, ribs, tenderloin, or liver.

By the 1930s the mountains had been overhunted, so wild game like rabbits, squirrels, and woodchucks were scarce. A lot of patience was required to kill even a squirrel. Still, now and then Dad would get lucky and kill something. After he had carried it home, Mom would clean the animal, boil it, roll it in flour, and fry it. Mom always made sure that the game meat was cooked well done. She used the drippings for gravy.

Because of Mom and Dad's hard work we were almost self-sufficient while we were living in the cove. A long time could pass between visits to the store. However, we did have to make hay while the sun shone, as they say. Mom probably worked harder than anyone I knew. She cooked, washed our clothes, and preserved most of our food. On top of this she helped Dad in the fields, particularly during the planting and harvesting seasons. When we kids were babies, she always had one of us tied to her back while she worked in the fields, just like the Indians depicted in photographs and paintings of the time. As we kids grew older, we also worked alongside Mom or Dad. We picked beans, berries, grapes, and nuts and helped in the garden and the fields. Life was physically hard, but it was also satisfying.

It was truly a very pleasant time for me. I especially loved
the berry picking, apple harvesting, and gardening.

As for our clothing Dad and us boys wore store-bought bib
overalls while Mom and the girls wore homemade dresses.
Mom was always worried about us kids getting sick, so
she made us wear store-bought long johns from October
to May, no matter how warm it might have been outside.
During the rest of the year we men wore nothing under
our overalls. In addition to all her other jobs Mom was also
our seamstress. She had a pedal sewing machine on which
she made shirts for Dad and us boys and dresses and un-
derclothes for herself and the girls. She got her cloth from
flour and animal feed sacks, which back then were made
from printed cloth that came in a variety of designs.

When it was clear and warm, Mom washed our clothes
on a washboard once a week. Once they had been scrubbed,
the clothes were boiled in a big cast-iron pot. Then they
were rinsed, wrung by hand, and hung on a clothesline to
dry. Mom usually did all the laundry herself. She even made
her lye soap from hog grease and wood ashes.

As it was, our clothes were washed about as much as we
were. We only bathed once a week in water that Mom had
heated on our kitchen stove. Usually we shared our bathwater, as both water and firewood were scarce, and we needed
to conserve them. In the winter our baths were even less
frequent. This might not have been very hygienic, but we
did not have running water, let alone a bathroom, and so
our house was very cold, and firewood could not be wasted

on heating the frigid water. All of our heat came from an old wood-burning stove from which you could only warm one side at a time, and then only if you were standing very close to it. While the bathwater was warm, it still left you cold when the bath was over.

In May we children took off our shoes and left them off until Mom made us put them back on in October. It sure felt good to take those shoes off in May, so good that when I started school, I would leave home every morning wearing shoes, just to please Mom. But once I got to the swinging bridge, they would come off, and I would hide them there so that I could continue on to school barefooted. On the way home I would reclaim my shoes and make sure I was wearing them before I saw Mom because I knew that Mom would get real mad if she knew that I did not wear shoes to school. And I knew better than to get Mom mad. Mom was often angry about something, so she was usually ready to take her anger out on one of us if we took the slightest step out of line.

Back then parents did not fret over spanking their children, and Mom sure did not have qualms about spanking us. She considered it to be her duty, and she seemed to enjoy it. Dad, on the other hand, took no joy in it, so he was happy to leave this task to Mom. Mom's choice switch was a long, tough, slim two-foot willow limb. Mom taught me in her own way that willow limbs make very good switches. We kids always tried to hide Mom's switch when she wasn't looking, but usually this would just make her madder than ever. She wanted to have her switch within arm's reach, and if she could not find it, she would send me out for a new one.

Picking out a switch was not easy; you could almost say that it was an art. I knew that I had to give Mom time to simmer down, but if I took too long Mom would just get madder and madder, and my punishment would only get worse. On top of this I had to get the right-sized switch. If it were too big, it would hurt too much. But if the switch were too small, it would just make Mom madder, and she might be provoked to the point that she would go get her own switch. You could bet that the switch she fetched would be perfect to the task.

Our first car was a 1931 two-door Chevrolet sedan. Mountain people really liked Chevrolets. We had little money for gas, so the car usually sat in the garage unless we really needed it, like when we would go to Whittier or Bryson City to shop or when we would visit Aunt Grace and Uncle Neal up on Goose Creek. Otherwise we walked everywhere. Because we did not drive her often, the old Chevy was in good shape. But still, we did not have that car long before Dad decided to trade her in for a newer car.

Jim Maney, Dad's uncle, sold stuff for a living, and he was pretty good at it. During the summer he accompanied trucks that hauled fruit around the mountains to help the drivers sell their produce. I always looked forward to Jim's visits. I thought that he was a lot of fun, and he always had a good story to tell. Most of all I liked it when he came up to the cove with a truckload of watermelons or Georgia peaches.

Uncle Jim also sold cars, and he knew that Dad wanted one. One day he drove into the cove with a gleaming black four-door 1934 Master Deluxe Chevrolet sedan. What a beautiful car. Dad and Mom decided to buy it on the spot. Uncle Jim accepted our old car as down payment, and Mom and Dad promised to make monthly payments on the remaining two hundred dollars. This might not sound like much, but it was a pretty deep hole to be in during the Depression on an Indian reservation.

Mom and Dad were grinning from ear to ear when Uncle Jim dropped the keys into Dad's hand. They heartily promised to make the payments. But they quickly learned that making that promise was a lot easier than making the payments. All winter long Mom and Dad worked like dogs to scrape the money together. They earned much of it by cutting pulpwood. Dad had a two-man crosscut saw. Standing in snow up to their ankles, Mom held onto one end and Dad onto the other, and they sawed furiously until they had sold enough pulpwood to meet that month's payment. The work was a backbreaking and miserable. The miserable weather made it even more so.

Eventually the misery of cutting pulpwood pushed Mom and Dad to try moonshining. They placed a thirty-gallon wooden tub behind the kitchen stove, filled it with something, covered the tub with cheesecloth, and let it sit. After a few days the tub began to smell so good that I would crawl behind the stove and just sit there drawing in that wonderful odor. When I asked Mom what was in the tub, she said that she was making vinegar. I might have been young, but I knew the smell of Mom's grape-wine vinegar, and I knew that whatever was in the tub was not vinegar.

A couple of weeks later, on a Saturday evening, Gillian and Philip came to the cove carrying a mechanical contraption in a burlap sack. Gillian, Philip, Mom, and Dad went into the kitchen. We children tried to follow, but Mom and Dad sternly admonished us to stay out. I knew then that something very mysterious was unfolding in the kitchen. Every now and then I peeked in to see what they were doing. I saw that they had taken some of the mixture from the tub and put it in a big pot on the stove. Then they placed the mechanical contraption on top of the pot. I could also see that whatever it was they were up to was not going well. The contraption on the pot was leaking steam.

Mom and Dad were too busy fussing with the pot to notice that I had snuck into the kitchen. Although I knew nothing about moonshine, I could tell that they had big problems. They pushed the pot off the heat and took the mechanical contraption off the pot. Dad placed his big soldering iron inside the stove to heat it and tried to solder the holes in the contraption, but Dad's big old soldering iron would not get hot enough to melt the solder. Discouraged, late that night they gave up. They carried the mixture out to the backyard and dumped it into the branch that passed pretty close to Jim Parker's house on the way to the river. Then Gillian and Philip placed the leaky still back into the sack and walked back to Grandma's house. I know that

Mom and Dad were disappointed; they really needed the money. Now they had to go back to cutting pulpwood. Gillian and Philip could never do anything right.

The next morning Dad was out in the front yard when Jim Parker came up to the gate below our house. Jim asked Dad if he thought someone had been making whiskey somewhere up here in the cove. I know my Dad must have been a little worried because people were always going to jail for making moonshine. Dad emphatically denied that anyone was making whiskey in the cove. Then Jim said that the night before he smelled the strong odor of whiskey and that the smell seemed to be coming from up in the cove. Dad again insisted that he had not smelled anything and added that he knew for a fact that no one was up in the cove making whiskey. Dad said that he kept a close watch over the entire cove. He said he was sure that no one had slipped over the mountain into the cove to make whiskey. After all, Dad told Jim, there were so many better places to moonshine.

I think Dad was relieved when Jim said he had to be going, turned, and went on his way. Jim never asked Dad about the whiskey again. I think Jim knew that Mom and Dad had tried to make whiskey, and he did not mean any harm by asking Dad these questions. He was just warning Dad that if he were going to make whiskey in the cove, people would know about it. I bet that Jim had seen Gillian and Philip carrying the burlap sack on their way up to the cove.

That was the last time Mom and Dad tried to make moonshine. I have to say they must have really needed the money, because it was a brave thing for them to try to make whiskey so close to their neighbor's house.

It seems that mountain people, Indian and white alike, have always been poor, regardless of which political party was in charge in Washington. Even during the best of times money never seemed to find its way up into the North Carolina Mountains. It surely did not take the Great Depression for us mountain folk to have to work hard and have nothing to show for it. I will say, however, that once Roosevelt started his New Deal policies, the lives of us mountain folk improved immediately. It is somewhat ironic that this would be so, because the Indians, including my Dad, hated Democrats, and they hated no Democrat more than Franklin Delano Roosevelt himself.

However much they might have hated Roosevelt, they sure did love his work programs. For the first time almost everyone could find work. Dad got a job as a laborer with the Civilian Conservation Corps (CCC). This was the first steady job that he had since he married Mom. Dad shared his job, and he worked two weeks out of every four. Someone else took his job during the other two weeks. He earned fifteen dollars a month for the two weeks of work.

Most of the CCC work in Cherokee consisted of working on roads and trails and guarding against forest fires. After working for a while with the CCC as a laborer, Dad landed a job as fire warden for Birdtown. This was Dad's dream job. Each morning he left home with his fire rake on his shoulder. All he had to do was to walk the mountaintops keeping his eye out for smoke. He loved being out in the woods far away from his boss. The only supervision he had was a daily call to the Indian Agency, which he made from the principal's office at the Birdtown School. That was the only phone in Birdtown. Each day, during the midafternoon, Dad came by the cove. Then he and I would go down to Birdtown so that he could report in.

On this job Dad found himself doing exactly what he loved to do most of all. He would ramble around the woods looking for animals and wild bees and, of course, signs of smoke. He would drop in on friends with whom he would trade various items for game roosters, clocks, knives, and other things. The Indians loved to trade. Now and then he would come across a wild bee tree that he and my uncle Hartman would go back to for the honey.

Hartman was my uncle on my mother's side of the family. I always thought he was simple-minded and probably retarded. He did attend school for a little while, and Mom said he attended night school late in life, though I know that this is not true. Hartman was long dead during the time that Mom claimed he was in night school. Hartman never moved off the reservation, and as an adult he lived less than a mile from Cherokee, just below the Queen farm on the road to Birdtown. He lived in a shack down over a steep bank from the roadway on a bit of level land that lay on the bank of the Oconaluftee River. He shared his home with a woman named Maye, and they had several children together. Because Hartman and Maye never married, Mom and her sisters refused to accept Maye as a member of the family. This is why we never visited Hartman at his house. When Dad or Mom wanted to talk with him, Dad would stop the car on the edge of the road above Hartman's house, and Mom or Dad would get out of the car and call down to him. We children were never allowed to get out of the car. Instead we would sit quietly in the car, straining our necks to look down over the bank so that we could see what was going on at this sinful house. I never learned much about Hartman's children because I never met any of them. When I asked Mom about the kids I used to see down in his yard, she would jump on the defensive and claim that Hartman never had any children. She claimed that Hartman was not the father of Maye's children.

Hartman never had a meaningful job. During the 1930s Hartman made money by collecting scrap iron that he would sell to Japan. Between his visits to our house I would find and save small pieces of iron that Hartman would buy from me for a nickel. Hartman had little sense of responsibility, and like a free spirit he wandered around the reservation, spending a few nights here and a few nights there before going home. There were times that he would stay away from home for days on end. Sometimes he would come and stay with us for a few days, and Mom and Dad always welcomed him into our home. When he stayed with us he would cut firewood, weed the crops, and wander around the woods looking for bee trees.

I have fond memories of his visits. He was good-natured and got along well with us children, perhaps because his intellect was childlike. He spoke in short sentences just like a child. I last saw Hartman in 1967 at the Cherokee Fair, at the toilets on the hill above the stickball field. For some reason Hartman was hanging out up there. He recognized that I was related to him, but he could not remember how, nor could he remember my name. He called me Dugan that day. When he could not remember a person's name that's what Hartman would call them, Dugan.

While the situation in the cove might have been great for Dad, it was less than ideal for Mom, and it was not long before she tired of living there. I really can't blame her. This was a far cry from the dreams that she once had of becoming a chorus girl and dancing on stage in New York City. By then these dreams were probably a distant memory, or perhaps she still had these dreams to fill the monotony of tending to Dad and us kids. I think that we were the only people she saw. To help Mom out, around 1940 Dad made a deal with his mother to build a house on Grandma's property in an old roadbed a little ways down the road from Grandma's house. He built a five-room house, a privy, a chicken house, and a small barn for our cows. We moved there, but it took Mom less than two years to tire of this house, so we moved back to the cove.

By the early 1940s, around the time Dad finished our house on the road, the war in Europe had begun to revive the economy, which ironically would take Dad away from the job that he loved so much. Now there were even more jobs in the mountains. Dad was able to get work at the Glenville Dam construction site and later at Fontana Dam.

These jobs were not in Cherokee, and Dad had to travel two hours each way to them, sitting on a wood-plank bench in the back of a flatbed truck. The truck had a tarp over the bed to shield the workers from the rain. Although the commute was miserable, the work was full-time, and it paid better than the CCC job.

Eventually Dad tired of the traveling, and he landed a job on the crew that was constructing the new bridge across the Oconaluftee River at Cherokee. After the bridge was finished, the contractor offered Dad a full-time position working on road projects near Asheville—an offer Dad turned down because he did not want to leave Cherokee. I doubt that Mom would have let him go away on a job anyway.

The highlight of the year was the first week in October, the week of the Cherokee Fair. The first Cherokee Fair was held in 1914 and was a huge success for everyone, the Indians, whites, and tourists alike. The fair was judged at that time to be the best in western North Carolina—even better than the Asheville fair. After such a booming debut the fair became an annual event. To me this was the most exciting week of the year. It was even better than Christmas, much better.

The fair began on Monday and ran for six days, ending the following Saturday at midnight. The fair included exhibits, midway rides, sideshows, restaurants, and Indian dancing and games. Like most of the Indians we always had something to exhibit: I think that each family that entered an exhibit received a free pass to the fair. Our exhibit was always small. We usually took plates of food and some of Mom's canned goods. I would search the woods for the prettiest persimmons I could find, which I would arrange on an exhibit plate.

Each year Aunt Grace and Uncle Neal ran a restaurant out of a simple two-room tin-roofed structure at the fair. The serving area was in the front room. It had counters on three sides, each with benches for the customers to sit on. The rear room, the kitchen, housed an icebox, a woodstove, and storage shelves. Grace and Neal always served hot dogs and hamburgers and sometimes bean bread, bean dumplings, chestnut bread, and other Indian food. I used to love how the aroma of the food hung over the fairgrounds. At about seven in the evening I would begin to get tired and cold, and I would always go to Grace's kitchen, where I would crawl into the warm cozy space behind the kitchen stove. Once I was warm and rested, I would head back out to the midway.

I was never interested in the Indian dancing and ball games. My friends and I would, at times, hang out around the Indian activities, but to be honest we were really interested in the activities in the midway, which was where we spent most of our time. There we encountered strange, mysterious, and exotic things, such as the Gypsy families with their big black cars and unusual dress. The Gypsy women would sit under a tent and tell fortunes while their children played nearby. I loved to stand and stare at them as they uncovered the secrets to people's lives, but I was always too shy to talk to them. They seemed to come from another world.

The midway also had many rides, such as the merry-go-round and the loop-the-loop. Of course there were also sideshows that featured the usual oddities and strip shows, the latter of which would draw the ire of preachers and the more religious Indians. Each year we could depend on these people to complain about the nudity, prompting the police to close down some of the strip shows or order the girls to show less of their bodies. My mom said that they did this only after all the men, including the policemen and preachers, had had a chance to see the show.

Once Dad and Mom took us to see the wild man who ate live chickens, which I thought was a horrible show. A stringy-haired man holding a live chicken in his hand danced around for a while, then bit into the neck of a chicken. He tore at the feathers and, supposedly, ate a little of the live chicken. To this day I am not convinced that he really ate the chicken. I did not like the show. But I did like the monkey show, where you could watch monkeys act like real people by doing tricks like driving little cars around a circular track. I always marveled at how smart the monkeys were. Now, after living all these years, I think those monkeys were indeed smarter than a lot of people.

When I got older, my friends and I would hang out around the strip shows. Each had a stage in front of the show tent where girls would dance around and give men a taste of what they could see if they would buy a ticket and come inside. We boys would stand around the outside stage watching the girls' sexy dances and listening to the barkers promise that the girls would show much more inside the tent. We were never lucky enough to go into the tent, but we always tried to peek.

I did go with some of my friends to see a hermaphrodite, a big ugly woman (or man) in a dirty old robe. The show promised that this creature would display both male and female sex organs. This creature said nothing, it just grunted now and then, and it did display both male and female sex organs, but not at the same time, so I could not quite figure out what I was looking at. When I looked over and saw a skinny little old man with a wide grin on his face, I decided that we had seen the real thing. The skinny little man, with a wry grin, assured us that the creature sure had both of them. He seemed happy and acted as if he had gotten his money's worth. Perhaps we got our money's worth too, but I still think that I wasted twenty-five cents.

On the Sunday morning after the last day of the fair, our family would go to the fairgrounds and help Aunt Grace and Uncle Neal tear down their restaurant. The midway and side-show area would already be empty, except for the scraps of paper and waste that littered the area. The rides and shows would already be on their way to the next fair. I always felt sad when I thought of the long year ahead until the next fair, and I envied the fair workers and entertainers. I used to dream of being old enough to travel with them to the next town.

The fair attracted tourists from all over. One year a young lanky redhead named George Willis came to the fair from Jacksonville. Mom's younger sister, Madge, was working in Grace's restaurant when George stopped by for a hotdog. It seems that before he had finished his meal, Madge was in love. George stayed with us while he was attending the fair and courting Madge, which makes me think that he might have struck up an acquaintance with Madge because he needed a place to stay. George would sleep all afternoon so that he would be well rested for a hard night at the fair. He sure could snore. It was not long after his visit that George and Madge got married, and she followed him to Jacksonville.

Grace and Neal Owl were my favorite aunt and uncle. Grace was my mother's older sister. Before she married Neal Owl, she had one daughter from a previous marriage. Until about 1947 Neal and Grace lived on a small lot in the Goose Creek area of the reservation. When the Soco Gap highway to Asheville opened in the late 1940s, the Indian Agency parceled out one-acre lots along the highway to Indians who applied for the land. Grace and Neal were lucky and obtained a flat plot that fronted on the main highway and backed up on Soco Creek, not far from the present site of the Casino hotel. They built a small house on the plot and moved from Goose Creek. Like most of the reservation Soco had no utilities, so Grace, Neal, and everyone else who lived along the road had to carry water from a spring in the woods on the other side of Soco Creek. To make it easier to get to the spring, Neal built a simple bridge. He cut down a large tree and let it fall across the creek. He trimmed all the limbs from the tree and then nailed some narrow boards on the tree to form a footbridge. The bridge extended some thirty feet across the creek, about five feet above the rocks lying in the shallow water below.

Being a lazy sort, Neal did not add a handrail. This made trips across the bridge hazardous, especially when the planks were wet or icy. Shortly after Neal completed the bridge, Grace slipped off and fell to the rocky creek bed. She sustained an injury that rendered her a cripple, and she had to use a walker for the rest of her life.

Not long after that Neal contracted typhoid—probably from the polluted spring water. I went to see Neal just before he died. When I arrived, he was sitting in the kitchen before a mirror, trying to shave. He felt so bad that I did not stay long. I doubt that he even knew that he had typhoid. After his death Grace continued to live in Cherokee, and eventually she remarried. After she remarried she sold her place on Soco and moved to a small house located farther up toward Soco Gap, where she lived until she died in 1970. Grace was a highly praised maker of Indian crafts. Her specialty was braided wool rugs, some of which, along with some other items, are in the Smithsonian Institution's collection of Indian arts and crafts.

My dad's sister Lula married George Howard and followed him to Kannapolis, where George worked in a textile mill. Every now and then they would visit us, and once they came up to the cove with a mongrel sheepdog named Rex. From day one Rex seemed to be at home in the cove, but he never wanted to come into our house. This makes me think that Rex must have been an Indian dog, as Indian dogs were outside dogs too. If you took an Indian dog into your house, the dog would become scared and pee on the floor.

Rex loved to bring the cows from the pasture at milking time. All Dad had to do was go out into the yard and say, "Go get 'em, Rex," and Rex was on his way. In a few minutes Rex would have the cows at the barn. Most of the time, however, Rex would just lie around. Rex and I spent a lot of time just hanging out together. Whenever I went into the yard, he would be there waiting for me. He was my constant companion.

Around this time Dad came home with an RCA Victrola record player, which I loved to listen to. I would stand on a chair, wind the record player, play hillbilly records, and sing along with the music. Rex would come onto the porch, stand at the front room window, and howl as if his heart were breaking. We were a good duet.

Rex was a good dog, but he was not a silly happy dog like some dogs that jump all over you, lick you up and down, and run madly around. He always seemed serious and sad. He used to sit there looking up to the head of the cove with a faraway, melancholy look in his eyes, as though something bore on his mind, like he was lonesome. I would not have been surprised if he was, because he never saw another dog. He just had my sister Betty and me to play with.

One day I went out looking for Rex, and I could not find him. He had disappeared. After a couple of days he returned and seemed happy to be home. However, after a few days he disappeared again for a couple of days, and once again, after a few days, he returned. Then one day he left and never came back. Dad thought that he must have gone over the mountain to the prison at Whittier. So one day we went to the prison to ask about him. The prison guard said that Rex had been coming to the prison and had taken up with one of the prisoners. The guard added that the prisoner liked Rex very much and that he fed Rex from his plate. The guard said that when the prisoner completed his term he took Rex with him. We never saw Rex again.

Over the years I have thought a lot about old Rex, and I have tried to figure out what was going on in his head when he was living with us in the cove. I could not believe that a dog would leave a little boy and go off with a grown man. As I got older and I watched the Lassie movies, I would compare Rex with Lassie. Lassie would never run off and leave a little boy. Lassie would brave all kinds of danger just to get home to be with her little master. Rex was no Lassie. Now that I am older, I think that I know why Rex abandoned me. I have heard that a dog is only loyal to the last person who feeds him. But I think old Rex was smarter than that. I think Rex was only loyal to the person who last fed him best. I guess old Rex did not like the table scraps of bread and gravy that we fed him. We never threw any meat into the scrap bucket, and dogs love meat. I am sure the prisoner gave Rex the best food on his plate, and Rex got used to eating high on the hog. So I guess Rex wanted to stay with me, but he wanted good food more.

The government built a small ill-equipped hospital at Cherokee in 1916. Before then Indians had to go to Bryson City or Whittier to see a doctor, and the poor condition of the roads made prompt medical care impossible. Many Indians found it easier to rely on local folk healers. Even after the hospital had opened, a few Indians continued to consult with these healers or sought no treatment at all. Even Uncle Neal, who had typhoid in the late 1940s, did not go to a doctor for treatment.

Under these conditions even a minor infection could be life threatening. Many Indians died of smallpox and other preventable diseases even after vaccines for these diseases were widely available. Nevertheless, slowly, Indians accepted modern medicine, and by the early 1930s most Indians sought medical care at the Cherokee Hospital.

By the time I was born, the Cherokee Hospital was well equipped, and medical care was free for all Indians. The care was good, probably better than any medical service in North Carolina west of Asheville. Doctors like Dr. Johnson, who was the resident physician in the 1930s, worked hard to raise the level of health care. He gladly made house calls. All my siblings and I were born in the Cherokee Hospital with Dr. Johnson in attendance.

By 1932 the Indian Agency was working hard to encourage preventative medicine on the reservation. Nurses made visits to schools and homes, where they taught food safety and personal hygiene. They also gave shots during these visits. However, even in the 1930s, like many Indian families, our family did not take advantage of these vaccinations. Before we entered school, we children had only had the diphtheria vaccine. Grandma Lambert and Dad, like most of the lay preachers in the mountains, believed that vaccinations were instruments of the devil.

Nevertheless, once we started school, neither we children nor our parents had any say in the health care that the Indian Agency provided to us. Nurses made monthly visits to the schools, provided examinations, and gave shots. I always dreaded it when I saw the nurses arrive. I knew that it meant that I was going to get a shot.

The most painful procedure was the tuberculosis test, for which a nurse stuck a needle into the front of my forearm and pushed the plunger until a bubble emerged on my arm at the point of the needle. About a week later the nurse returned and examined the bubble to read the test result. I never could figure out exactly what that test was all about, but I did know that the test sure did hurt.

My family came down with the same illnesses that affected all the Indians on the reservation: colds, the flu, measles, chicken pox, mumps, intestinal problems, and boils. The only serious illness to affect our family was when Betty came down with diphtheria. Dr. Johnson quarantined our family until her condition improved. Against Grandma Lambert's objections he gave us all diphtheria shots. Other very common health problems among the Indians on the reservation and the mountain people were TB, head lice, alcoholism, typhoid, scarlet fever, whooping cough, pneumonia, and accidental injuries.

Grandma Lambert would eventually die from TB. We had a close relationship with her, and it was a miracle that none of our family members contracted the disease as well. This was probably because she was very careful. She only used a dedicated set of dishes, a plate, a fork, a cup, and a spoon, that she kept far away from the other dishes on the sink drain board. As an added precaution she did not cook. Her son Gillian usually cooked and cleaned for her. When we ate at her house, Mom cooked and cleaned up for us.

Indians used many home remedies for colds, the flu, and aches and pains. My mom treated the flu and colds with aspirin and catnip or sassafras tea. She treated chest congestion and boils with aspirin and poultices. Mom made the poultices by wrapping a lump of hot oatmeal in a thick cloth. She placed the poultice on the affected area of the body. Surprisingly, these treatments seemed to work quite well.

Alcoholism was a big problem on the reservation and, along with guns and knives, posed real health hazards to Indian families. I am convinced that the fact that alcohol was illegal actually promoted alcoholism. Anyone who bought a jar of whiskey thought that they had to drain it immediately or else they might be arrested. I know that my father had an alcohol problem when he was a young man, but neither he nor my mother used alcohol after we were born. Our family never suffered the ill effects of alcohol abuse.

We never went more than a few miles from home. It just did not occur to us to travel, and besides, we could not afford to travel anyway. Until 1943, when we moved to Tennessee, we children had never been farther from home than the Newfound Gap on the Tennessee border, about fifteen miles from Cherokee. Instead our social life consisted of visits with relatives, and since we had so many living nearby, it was easy to find someone to visit on any given Sunday. This was the only day when Mom and Dad didn't have to work. Although Mom and Dad were not religious, they did respect the Sabbath as a day of rest. We regularly visited Grandma Lambert, Grandpa Smith, and Grace and Neal.

Although I did not enjoy being around Grandpa Smith, I did like visiting his house. Grandpa Smith and Estaline had a lot of children, and as soon as we arrived, we kids would disappear, and we would not return until we were called to go home.

I also enjoyed visiting Grandma Lambert. Her house had a narrow stairway that led from the living room to the attic. I used to spend hours in the attic going through all the mysterious things that were stored there. Usually Philip or Gillian would take us fishing, which was a lot of fun. They spent most of their time sitting around on Grandma's front porch picking the guitar and singing hillbilly songs. I don't remember either of them as having been any good, but I later learned that Philip must have been better than I thought. I read an obituary in the *Cherokee One Feather* of a man who had played in a band with Philip. They toured around the South and had steady work at a radio station in Charlotte. That was probably the closest either Gillian or Philip ever came to having a regular job. They made most of their money helping Grandma sell moonshine.

We also visited Aunt Grace and Uncle Neal about once a month, which I enjoyed because Grace and Neal were always so happy and Grace would usually cook us a big meal. Grace was a skillful craft maker, and she was always working on interesting projects that she would show us. Since Neal was so lazy, Grace's craft making was the family's main source of income.

Our relatives also visited us. In fact, as most of our relatives did not have steady jobs, we could expect someone to drop in for lunch on any given day. Hartman often came by for lunch. Once Grandpa Smith and his family showed up at our home and moved in. They just settled in and gave no indication that they planned to move out. While we children loved having Grandpa Smith's children living with us, it did not take long for Dad to tire of the situation. At the end of his rope, Dad told Grandpa that a place at the head of Kate Lambert Branch was for sale for seventy-five dollars. Grandpa took the hint, and he and his family moved shortly thereafter.

For a while Mom and Dad played a card game with our neighbors called setback. The players placed bets with matchsticks. I never learned the rules, but they did play the game with a regular deck of playing cards. My parents always had a good time playing this game, and they would often play it well into the night. For some reason, around

1940 Mom and Dad quit playing setback and banned playing cards from our house. Maybe they decided that cards
were sinful. Later, as we children grew older, Mom and
Dad allowed us to play old maid and rook.

I really enjoyed listening to our record player, but after a while Dad traded our record player away. I was sad to
see it go, but soon afterward Dad bought a big floor radio
that required five dry-cell batteries of various sizes. The
batteries were expensive, so we used the radio sparingly.
The radio brought a new world into our house. We could
hear the *Grand Ole Opry* from Nashville, the *Mid-Day Merry-
Go-Round* from Knoxville, and programs from many other
faraway places like Del Rio, Texas. We listened to boxing,
Lum and Abner, and Amos and Andy.

The first Baptist missionaries began to work with the Cherokee in the early 1800s, when the Cherokee Nation was
still in the East. By the early 1900s the Baptist Church
was well established on the Qualla Boundary, and for the
most part the Cherokee Baptist churches were run by Indians. There were other denominations on the reservation as well, among them Methodists and Quakers. And
of course there were plenty of plain old Fundamentalists
who did not owe an allegiance to any denomination. Most
of these churches had neither regular pastors nor regular
services. We Indians just did not have the money back then
to employ a full-time preacher.

As for our family we rarely went to church when we were
living in Cherokee. We went to the Birdtown Church a few

times, and every year we went to the Methodist Church for the Christmas party. I think that we only went to the Christmas party because they handed out free presents. Church was just not that important to my parents, even though they thought that they were religious. But I guess that my parents were not all that different from everyone else on the reservation, as most churches sat empty on most Sundays.

Also similar to my parents, it was part of the culture in the mountains to claim to be religious. In fact most men would acquire the title of Reverend at some point in life. This was not hard to do. It could be achieved by taking a short home-study course or by simply purchasing a certificate. This would hardly qualify them as biblical scholars, but it would give them license to deliver some fiery sermons. By reading the *One Feather* I have learned that some of my boyhood friends, just like their fathers, became reverends in their later years. Both my grandpa Jack and my grandpa Smith were lay preachers. As for Dad he became a preacher at the age of sixty-five.

Usually only adults had any interest in religion. Despite this many teenagers also attended services, particularly the revivals that were held in the summer. At dusk, as I used to walk through the church parking lot during these services, I would see many of these teenagers in their cars making out with their girlfriends. I guess that it would be quite a few years before they intended to assume the title of Reverend.

Because our churches could not afford to pay full-time preachers, most had to hold other jobs. This made it hard for them to preach every Sunday, so most would focus their pastoral efforts on revivals, which I always found to be impressive events. One preacher would start out slowly, gradually building up the pace. Once he was soaked with perspiration, another preacher would get up, and the first preacher would sit down while wiping the sweat from his forehead. They would go on like this for hours, not missing a beat as they passed the pulpit between them. Their main message was not very deep or hard to understand. In a nutshell they were telling everyone to give all the money they could to the Lord. Now and then someone in the audience would rise to their feet and testify how the Lord had made them rich after they started giving 10 percent of their income to the Lord. The preachers never failed to pass the collection plate at each revival meeting, but unfortunately for the preachers, the congregations were always poor, and the collections were always meager.

One of the more interesting events that I saw at the revivals were young children, some as young as twelve, who would preach. These "child preachers" were always accompanied by an older preacher who was really in charge. Nevertheless, this child would be right up at the pulpit preaching hell-fire sermons, and the audience would marvel at how well he "knew" the Bible.

The revivals lasted a long time, sometimes as long as two months. Some revivals moved around the reservation, drawing in the same people at each meeting, year after year. At times, however, newcomers would show up at the revival meeting, hoping to have their souls saved. The preachers were always happy to oblige.

The preachers always delivered a simple message of salvation. The general pattern was for a person to get religion, then they would backslide, and then they would get religion again. Then, once again, they would backslide, and the cycle would continue. At times even the preachers would backslide. At one revival meeting I learned that during past the week one of the preachers, who had a large family, had run off with someone else's wife. It was not long before the preacher and the errant wife ran short of money and returned to Cherokee. After they returned, the congregation decided to go to the preacher's house and hold a prayer meeting, re-save him, and make it possible for him to return to the pulpit. Sure enough, the preacher was right back in the pulpit at the next revival meeting. During the next few meetings the preacher devoted a lot of time to telling the story of his transgression and how the Lord came to his rescue. I think the congregation liked hearing all the sordid details.

Preachers baptized new converts during the summer at the riverbank. They said that you had to be baptized in the same fashion that Jesus had been baptized in the river Jordan. That is, you had to be fully immersed. In their view any other type of baptism would not work, and worse, it was the work of the devil. They also believed that it was a waste of time and sinful to baptize babies and children.

You had to be old enough to know right from wrong before you could do it.

True preachers never prepared a sermon, not even an
outline of one. Rather they believed that sermons had to be
inspired by God, as though the sermon was not from them,
but rather they were but a vessel for the voice of God. This
usually meant that the sermons were little more than an in-
coherent, randomly strung-together hodgepodge of words.
But I guess that the real message was not in the words, but
in their fiery delivery. And this fiery delivery they could do
quite well. So well, in fact, that I indeed felt like it was the
angry voice of God that was filling the revival tent. The sermons were usually about Paul, Solomon, and God. The congregation loved the Old Testament message of an eye for
an eye, and they agreed wholeheartedly with Paul's harsh
messages about life. These mountain people did not like
to think very much about Jesus's message of love and for-
giveness. It just did not fit into how they thought.

When a revival service was nearing its end, the preacher
would invite all the sinners who were present to come forward so that they could be saved. Some people at each service seemed to have a sixth sense that drew them toward
people who wanted to be "saved." Two or three of these
people would gather around the poor sinner and begin to
work on him. If the sinner really wanted to be saved, these
people would have him kneeling at the altar in no time.
They would gather around the sinner and start praying, and
they would continue praying, sometimes for a long time
if the sinner was resisting. Some of the people would get

carried away, and they would start dancing, shouting, and speaking in tongues. After a while "the holy spirit" would settle on the sinner, and the sinner would start crying. The sinner would cry for a while, and then he would jump up, shout, and declare that he was a changed person, thanks to God. At around eleven in the evening the service would end, and everyone would go home happy that one more person was on their way to heaven.

The saved person would go home believing that his life had been changed. Sometimes these people really did appear to change, and many of them would eventually take up preaching themselves. However, the more common story was that the next morning the repentant sinner would find that he still faced the same old problems as he had faced the morning before. Before long he would become discouraged and backslide into his old ways.

As historian John Finger describes it, in the 1880s, after several failed attempts by the government to establish a school system for the Cherokees, the government appointed the Quakers to come to the reservation and oversee the schools. The Quakers did an outstanding job, but as has often happened, factions emerged within the tribe that thought that others could do a better job. Rather than be drawn into a fight that they could not win, the Quakers decided not to renew their school contract in 1892. At this point the U.S. government decided that it was ready to operate the schools.[2] This school system was still in operation when I entered school in 1939.

In the 1930s the reservation school system consisted of the Central High School at Cherokee and three remote grade schools—one in Birdtown, one in Big Cove, and one in Soco. The high school had boarding facilities and provided twelve grades of education, while the remote grade schools provided education through the sixth grade. All the area grade schools were day schools, and we children thought that the worst thing that could happen to us was that our parents would send us to boarding school. When Mom really wanted to get our attention, she threatened to send us to the Cherokee boarding school. Mom fostered this fear by telling us about how her father had sent her to boarding school.

This is not to say that the boarding school was all that bad. I say this in spite of the fact that today some Indians are very critical of the boarding school. Some even make up stories about how the government rounded up children in the 1930s and 1940s and forced them to go to the boarding school at Cherokee. None of these stories are true. Cherokee students who boarded did so at their parents' discretion. After the sixth grade in the 1930s students were bussed daily, at the government's expense, to the Cherokee high school.

The Indian Agency operated the schools under federal guidelines. The federal government paid the teachers' salaries and all other expenses. Each student received books, paper, pencils, and medical care. At the start of the school year each Indian child received a clothing issue that included a heavy wool coat, headgear, galoshes, coveralls, shoes, and socks. Without the clothing issue many Indian children could not have attended school because they would not have had clothes to wear. In the 1930s most Indian families were very poor.

The school provided each child with a tasty hot lunch each school day. At Birdtown we Indian students spent part of the school day working on the school farm, particularly during the spring planting and fall harvesting seasons. The school used the food we grew to supplement the food served to students at lunch. While the food was good, I still refused to eat the spinach. When they served spinach, the cooks would make me sit at the table until I ate it all. Usually I refused, and I would sit there and cry because I would miss playtime.

In the 1930s education was not very important to most of the Indians. It didn't help that the white schools were much better than the Indian schools. Children in the white schools started the first grade when they were six, whereas Indian students entered the baby class, what today is called kindergarten, when they were six and the first grade when they were seven. This made us Indian children feel that we were not as smart as white children. In addition the curriculum in the Indian school was not as challenging as that of the white school. This increased our insecurities. To make matters worse, the curriculum in the Indian schools emphasized health and hygiene instead of reading, writing, and arithmetic, highlighting the fact that many of us came from homes with poor hygiene and the notion that we weren't clean enough to learn. Every now and then they made us shower in the school bathrooms.

Overall, despite its shortfalls, the Indian school system served the Indians very well, and the school system was an asset for the students who took full advantage of all the opportunities that it offered. I would have to say that although our curriculum was worse, the physical infrastructure of our school was better than that of the neighboring white schools. The federal government generously funded the Indian school system. This generosity mirrored the generosity of the government's commodity food program, which used the school to distribute surplus food to Indians. Our family really looked forward to commodity day, and we certainly got our share—cheese, dried fruit, grapefruit, flour, oatmeal and cream of wheat, cereals, and other foods.

Similar to other Indians Mom and Dad did not think that education was very important. I guess that this is understandable. Dad only went to school through the ninth grade, and Mom the sixth grade, if that. When it came time for me to enter school in 1938, Mom would not let me go. She said that she could not stand to see me go off to school each day all by myself. I did not complain because I did not want to go to school anyway. However, in the spring of 1939 the Agency must have ordered my parents to enroll me in school, as I found myself enrolled in the baby class at Birdtown when I was almost seven years old. Betty, my younger sister, entered school at the same time. I guess Mom and Dad insisted on this so that I would not have to walk to and from school alone. The following September I started the first grade at the age of eight.

The school opened my eyes to a new world. I developed friendships with David Bradley, Jack Bradley, Charles George, and others. David, Jack, and I were the best of friends. We became very brave, and at the age of eight we took to chewing tobacco. A couple of times a week, during lunch recess, one of us would slip across the road to a store and buy a plug of chewing tobacco. The owner, who was usually half drunk on moonshine, saw nothing wrong with selling a plug of tobacco to an eight-year-old. To encourage our patronage he often gave each of us a penny piece of candy along with our plug. We preferred sweet tobacco, and we spent many lunch recesses chewing and spitting.

One day David bought a plug of the strongest tobacco I had ever tasted. I took a little chew and after a few minutes became so violently ill that I was not able to return to the classroom when lunch recess ended. I remained outside lying on the grass, feeling sicker and sicker as the minutes ticked by. Of course my teacher did not know why I was sick, so she let me recuperate on the grass. After a while I recovered and returned to class. That was my last chew of strong tobacco at Birdtown School.

About half of the Indian students at Birdtown School did not look like Indians. Many of us had a fair complexion and blond hair, and we really stood out surrounded as we were by many near full-blooded Indians. Because I was one of these fair students, some of the older darker students teased me, and I teased them right back. They would call

me some name like "whitey," and I would call them "nig-
ger." This would really make them mad. They would run
after me and threaten to cut off my neck. I would think
about them cutting off my neck, and I decided that they
meant to cut off my head twice. When these games began,
I would run to one of Grace's nieces, Bessie Owl, for protection. Bessie, who was a big girl, bigger than those boys,
would double dare them to touch me. Among those boys
who would chase me and threaten to cut off my neck was
Tom, who years later I would hire to stand in front of my
gift shop dressed as an Indian chief. He looked sufficiently
"Indian" for the job.

When it was warm, my schoolmates and I went barefoot
at school. On one warm day I was running around barefoot during recess, and I stepped on a small clock part.
The shaft stuck into the ball of my foot and went almost
all the way through my foot. Although the pain was ex-
cruciating, I did not cry because I did not want my teacher
to know. I did not want anyone to know because I knew
that if I said anything about the accident, I would have to
see a doctor. I pulled the thing out of my foot and suffered
the pain in silence.

The wound never stopped hurting, and a few days later
the pain was so bad that I had to tell Mom about the accident. When Dad got home from work, he took me straight
to the Cherokee Hospital to have my foot checked. The doctor said the wound was infected, and he gave me a shot and
said I would have to stay in the hospital until my foot healed.

The nurse placed me in a ward with a couple of boys who were a little older than I was. Being shy and scared, at the outset I didn't dare say anything to them. The two boys had some kind of bone disease, and they had been in the hospital for a long time, and they felt right at home there, and they were always having a good time. They had stacks of comic books, like Batman, Superman, Wonder Woman, and many others. I had never seen a comic book before. When the boys saw that I was curious about the comic books, they kindly let me read them.

Once I started reading the comic books, I could not stop. I was fascinated by them, and they provoked my imagination to run wild. The two boys, realizing that I was captivated, starting telling tales about the stories, and they convinced me that the stories were true. I was so entranced by the comic books that I could hardly sleep at night. When I left the hospital, the boys gave me a stack of comics to take home. When I arrived at home, Mom was not happy about the books, especially when I told her that the stories were about real places and people. She finally convinced me they were not true, but it took some time.

Mom was a very jealous person, and she continually accused Dad of philandering. You have to remember that Mom was very young, had several children by that time, and stayed home all day while Dad was out working. In addition events had occurred in her life, such as the early death of her mother, which made her jealous and suspicious. Each day when Dad returned home from work, Mom would accuse Dad of seeing other women. For the most part Dad seemed to enjoy these accusations. When Mom started accusing him, he would just sit there and grin. This had the same effect as throwing gasoline on a fire. Mom would go into a rage. Then Dad would say something, and Mom would get madder. Then Mom would say something back at Dad, and Dad would get madder. Then the fight would shift into high gear. Dad would immediately say that he was leaving and would grab his hat and coat, stand in the doorway, and continue the verbal fight.

I do not know where he thought he could go. Maybe he thought he could go to Grandma's house. We children never knew when the fight would end, and usually it would continue far into the night, after all us kids had gone to bed. Sometimes the fight would last into the next day, sometimes even longer.

Neither Mom nor Dad ever apologized to each other for the fights. I do not know why they could not find it in themselves to say, "I am sorry." Rather, to end the fight they would slowly ease off each other. They would say nothing for a while, and then Dad would say something not pertaining to the fight and Mom would give a civil answer. When we children heard this, we would rejoice inwardly that the fight was finally over. Nevertheless, we children knew that we could not relax for long; we knew it would not be long until a new fight erupted. You see, I can't say that my family was very warm to one another. I never heard my parents tell each other that they loved one another. In fact they never even bothered to tell us children that they loved us.

The strained relationship between Mom and Dad reached the point where the most trifling comment by one or the other would send the other into a rage. Mom and Dad were too selfish and dense to admit that our family had a problem, and unfortunately, this quarreling continued until Dad died in 1993. And after that Mom started quarrelling with her children. Sometimes I think that Mom and Dad enjoyed and looked forward to fighting.

We kids, however, did not enjoy the fighting. When Mom and Dad fought, we children were scared to death. It didn't matter to us that our parents were not exchanging wallops; just hearing their vicious insults was bad enough. During the fight Dad would always threaten to leave, and I guess that we kids were really scared that he would make good on this threat. Even during the calm periods, when Mom and Dad were not fighting, we kids had to live in fear that a fight would begin.

It's hard for me to say what this fighting did for Mom and Dad, but I know that it did nothing but create problems for us kids. We learned that one way to stop the fighting was for one of us to pretend to be sick. And then once we had made this claim, we had to find a way to keep up the charade—which in itself is an illness. I think that this fighting also made us wet our beds until we were at least ten or eleven.

Nightmares were by far the worst effect of the fighting. These weren't your ordinary nightmares. These nightmares would cause us to wake up in a fearful tremble and in a trance that would last for as long as an hour. After it was over, we would be drained, terrified, and confused. Neither Mom nor Dad knew how to handle these night-mares. All they could do was hold the child in their arms until the awful episode had passed.

We were all affected by the nightmares, but I think Donald, the youngest of us, was affected the most. I spent many nights holding my youngest brother, Don, until he recovered. Don grew to be a nervous and high-strung man. In the past few years he prematurely contracted Parkinson's disease and had to be confined to an old folks' home. I can't help but think that Mom and Dad's fights made him this way. Even today I still cannot get those useless fights out of my mind.

On a bright sunny Sunday in December 1941 I was standing next to the kitchen steps at our house on the road when my uncle Sibbald, on his way to Birdtown, called up to me and told me that the Japanese had bombed Pearl Harbor and the United States had entered World War II. At first I thought, "So what?" What happened far away never seemed to make a difference to us. But this time it was different. That attack on Pearl Harbor changed our lives forever.

The first draftees for the war were eager idealistic young men in their late teens and early twenties who could not wait to go into battle. After the first horde of draftees marched into battle and died, the country found that the supply of boys in their teens and twenties was limited, and the age for the draft rose rapidly. Despite this Dad just drifted along, never believing that the draft age would rise into the thirties and threaten him. He was wrong. While we were living in the cove in 1942, the draft age inched to the mid-twenties and then very rapidly into the late twenties. This convinced Dad that the draft was going to get him if he stayed in Cherokee working at nonessential jobs.

Dad started looking for ways to avoid the draft. His talents and interests were mostly in the area of farmwork, and luckily, the government had placed farmworkers high on the list of men eligible for deferments. So Dad started looking for work on a large farm. He traveled to Richland, near Jacksonville, in search of work. He went to see a farm owner who was looking for a sharecropper to work his farm. At this job Dad would have earned a share of the farm profits and nothing more. Dad did not like the risk that this would have entailed and came home.

Then he checked on another job in Tennessee, near Mentor, a small rural community about eleven miles south of Knoxville and two miles from the town of Alcoa. Dad was pleased that this farm was not too far from Cherokee. Victor Hultiquist, the city manager of Alcoa, owned the farm. This job paid a salary and a share of the farm profits. Dad would receive seventy-five dollars a month and one week of vacation a year. Dad would also receive 15 percent of the profits of cattle sales and 25 percent of produce sales. At that time seventy-five dollars a month sounded like a fortune, and we were very happy. Even Mom was happy about the move. Victor gave us a farmhouse rent-free and provided us, at no cost, all the firewood we needed. He allowed us to use the chicken house for our chickens and the free pasture and barn for our cows. We could use the farm-grown hay and corn to feed our cows, chickens, and pigs. He also provided us with two or three fields for our gardens. To us this seemed a very good deal.

Tennessee

The cove was clear and cold on that January morning when we packed our few belongings and loaded them on the bed of a stake-body truck for the trip to Tennessee. We were heading for Victor Hultiquist's farm. Dad said that the tires on our 1934 Chevy were in no condition to make the trip, so he stored the car in our log cabin garage. As it was wartime the military needed all the rubber it could get. That made it almost impossible for poor people like us to buy new tires.

We pulled out of the cove at about nine in the morning. Mom, Dad, and Don rode up front in the cab with the driver. The rest of us kids rode in the back on the truck-bed with all of our stuff. When we got to Cherokee, Mom, Betty, Don, and I climbed off the truck and into the bus to Knoxville. Dad, my brother Sibbald, and my sister Helen continued the trip in the truck cab.

This trip to Tennessee was an adventure for everyone. We kids had never been farther from Cherokee than Newfound Gap. That day we were going far past Newfound Gap. We were going all the way to Knoxville, the home of the *Midday Merry-Go-Round*, our favorite hillbilly music radio program.

I got on the bus and took an aisle seat next to Betty. Mom and Don took the seats across the aisle. I could not contain my excitement. I spent the whole trip looking out the side windows and sticking my head into the aisle so I could see through the windshield. I wanted to see everything.

Mom did not want me to act like I had just walked off a farm, which of course I had. Whenever I poked my head into the aisle to catch a glimpse of Tennessee through the windshield, Mom would tell me to quit acting like a fool. I would pull myself back into my seat, but a few minutes later curiosity would get the best of me, and in no time I would be looking down the aisle again, staring through the large windshield off into Tennessee. Mom would tell me once again to quit acting like a country fool.

The scenery and the sights along the highway thrilled me. When we arrived at the Knoxville bus station, Dad and the truck were waiting for us. We older four children got back onto the truckbed, and Mom, Dad, and Don climbed into the cab with the driver. We took off down Highway 411 toward Maryville. About halfway to Maryville we turned right onto Topton Road, which we followed for five miles. Then we turned right onto the Hultiquist farm road. This was a very good gravel road, better than the Topton Road. It curved to the left down a hill, then around a right-hand curve, went over a culvert lake crossing, and rose gently up to our house and then on up a steep slope to Victor Hultiquist's big two-story house. Our old house was about a half mile from Topton Road and a quarter mile from Victor's house.

By the early afternoon the driver had parked the truck in the front yard of our new home, and we began unloading our meager belongings. The first thing Dad did was to set up the stove and start a fire. The house was very cold. At about four in the afternoon, as Mom was building a fire in the fireplace, a distinguished old gentleman smoking a big long cigar opened the front door and came into the front room. It was Victor, our landlord and boss. He paid us a greeting and asked if there was anything he could do. My mother told him that everything was under control. Then he spun around, walked out of our house, got in his car, and drove up the road to his house.

Eventually, Mom got the fire going in the fireplace. However, we quickly learned that the fireplace did not heat the house very well. Later Dad solved this problem by installing our wood-burning stove from the cove in the front room. The next day Dad and the driver took the truck back over the Smoky Mountains to Cherokee to fetch our livestock.

I was in hog heaven. This was not like our little patch of land in the cove over in Cherokee. This was a real farm with spacious fields, a big barn, and horses. For now at least I loved everything about it.

The old Hultiquist farm lay on the east side of a low mountain. To the west lay the Tennessee River and to the east Topton Road. A steep cliff rose three hundred feet straight up from the Tennessee River to the top of a low mountain. The farm's north boundary was marked by a creek that cut through that low mountain and drained a broad valley into the Tennessee River. This broad valley stretched for about two miles north to south, along the base of the mountain. When we moved to the farm, the Fort Loudoun power project was nearing completion, and in the summer the floodgates were closed and the water started filling the valley. The lake filled much of the broad valley, from just past Victor's farm road to more than one mile to the north. I watched with fascination as the water slowly rose.

Once the lake reached capacity, Dad built a small boat dock that floated on fifty-five-gallon steel oil drums. This is where Victor kept his boat. The dock was U shaped and had an A-frame compartment to cover and protect the outboard motor. Victor's boat was a sixteen-foot runabout with a windshield. The outboard engine had about thirty horsepower, which gave it a very peppy performance. Roughly once a week during the summer Victor would take the boat for a run around the lake. When he came to the farm, Victor also did a lot of fishing and was kind enough to leave his fishing gear at the boat dock for me to use.

The farm had five houses: Victor's house; our house; two houses where the farm road intersected with Topton road; and the Hicks' house, which was just about in the middle of the farm. Except for Victor's house the houses on the farm reminded me of our house in the cove. Of all of these houses our house was probably the best, but still, there was no comparison between our house and Victor's.

Victor's house, the largest and the grandest, had two stories and a full basement and was built from large bricks. It had four rooms downstairs—a kitchen, a dining room, a living room, and a library—and four bedrooms upstairs. A wide brick deck on the ground floor extended around the library, living room, and dining room. The house had cedar, wormy chestnut, and walnut paneling. There was a coal bin and a hand-fired furnace in the rear of the basement. Dad and I had to keep the fires burning all winter. We also had to clean the ashes from the furnace. Victor's water came from a nearby deep well.

Victor's house was about two hundred feet above the lake and surrounded by a broad green lawn. A field of alfalfa hay rolled down to the lake from the lower front lawn. There are few views that compare to that which you saw when you looked east from Victor's house across the lake to the foothills of the Smoky Mountains. The road to his house approached from the south through a patch of woods. Victor later extended the road around and below the house, back through the patch of woods and out to where it intersected with the road in front of our house. To the north of his house a steep embankment dropped off from the road to a sinkhole that must have been more than a hundred feet in diameter and about thirty feet deep. His garage was in the rear, across the road from the kitchen door. Victor's rock flower garden lay to the south of the garage. This was his pride and joy.

Our house sat well on the land. It was perched on a knoll, and several tall trees shaded the front yard. The house was a small white weatherboard house with a living room, bedroom, kitchen, and dining room. There was a small entry porch on both the front and back. Rainwater drained from the roof into a cistern that was equipped with a hand pump.

The yard sloped gently away from the house on the left side for seventy-five feet to a field. This is where we planted our garden. Our privy sat on the edge of the garden. The yard on the right side sloped down toward a drainage ditch that ran from the fields near the barn. Our front yard was mostly bare, hard, red clay. It rose gently to a knoll where the tall shade trees stood.

Dad added a second bedroom, a small hall, and space for an indoor bathroom. He installed a pipe that carried water from Victor's well to our kitchen. Dad never finished the bathroom, so he used that space for storage and as a place to cure hog meat.

Our first year on the farm was very good. Compared to how we were living in Cherokee, this was hog heaven. Although even back then seventy-five dollars a month was not much, it was a lot more than Dad had ever earned, and we never needed to spend much. Life on the farm was so good that, except to go to school, we didn't have to leave during the first seven months we were there. There was even a flatbed truck that came to our front yard loaded with groceries each week. Of course I guess that we might have stayed on the farm because we did not have a car.

The farm had about 200 acres, of which 80 were in cultivation and 120 were reserved for pasture and woodland. We had an excellent barn. It had a full loft, five stalls, and a corncrib. A chicken house extended along east side of the barn. Dad built a pigpen in a wooded area below the barn.

The farm was well equipped. We had a plow, a spike harrow, a rotary harrow, a hay mover, a hay rake, a corn planter, and a wagon. The farm also had a one-horse cart and a one-horse cultivator plow. We had all the hand tools we needed: hoes, rakes, and pitchforks. We had two horses, and later Victor would purchase a Ford tractor.

Just below the Hicks' house the farm had a very good spring. The farm had two or three alfalfa hay fields. In midsummer the alfalfa fields were beautiful, with light green plants and purple flowers waving in the Tennessee breeze. We mowed each field at least twice a year.

The farm had a good orchard with about six apple trees, two cherry trees, and a couple of pear trees. The apple and pear trees were in a cornfield on the upper side of the barn, and the cherry trees were in a pasture above the cornfield. The cherry trees grew wild throughout the farm, and we used the small cherries from these trees to make jelly. Strawberries, blackberries, raspberries, and dewberries also grew wild in great abundance. We had just about as much fruit as we had in the cove.

There was a strawberry farm about two miles from our house where each spring Betty, Helen, and I picked strawberries that we could sell for five cents a quart. We could easily pick twenty quarts each morning. Back then a dollar for a morning's work was not bad, particularly when we could also eat all the strawberries we wanted.

We were on a beautiful well-equipped farm and lived in a good house. The farm had unbounded potential, and as this was the middle of World War II and produce was in short supply, we were primed to make a lot of money. Unfortunately, we did not know how to make money, and we ended up not making any.

I look back now and dream about what we could have achieved if only we knew how to do it. The farm was on the newly created lake and had plenty of water. If we had a small pump and a short length of pipe, we could have irrigated our fields. Sadly, we never even thought of this, and we watched hopelessly as our crops shriveled up and died during droughts.

Victor, our boss, had no plans for making money with the farm. He earned his living as the city manager of Alcoa, Tennessee, a position he held for twenty-nine years. This was a very good job. Victor and Mrs. Hultiquist lived in a large house on the edge of the city park that, I am sure, Alcoa had built and furnished for him. Consistent with his status as Alcoa town manager, Victor drove a 1941 blue four-door Buick Sedan.

Victor was a distinguished gentleman, and at six feet he looked the part. Normally he was reserved, but at times he could be quite talkative. He was almost bald, and what little hair he had was gray. His round face was matched by a full, if not fat physique. He wore glasses and was seldom without a cigar in his mouth.

Mrs. Hultiquist was matronly, very friendly, and Victor's willing slave. She came to the farm with Victor a couple of times each weekend, where they would entertain invited guests. Mrs. Hultiquist took some interest in us kids, and sometimes she would bring us old magazines to read. We really liked the *National Geographic* magazines. One year she and Victor drove to Mexico during their summer vacation. When they returned, she gave each of us kids a little clay turtle. Years later I visited Mexico and saw the same little clay turtles for sale for five cents each. The Hultiquists really knew how to look after their money.

Before they moved to Alcoa, Victor was town manager of Calderwood, Tennessee, a small ALCOA company town deep in the mountains near the North Carolina–Tennessee border. This town once housed more than three thousand men who were building dams at Calderwood and other locations further up the Little Tennessee River. When the Calderwood Dam was complete, ALCOA, the company, offered Victor the job in the town of Alcoa.

Around 1920 the Aluminum Company purchased thousands of acres of choice farmland along Highway 411 in Blount County. On part of this land the company constructed three plants and the town of Alcoa. The company used the remaining land lying between the plants as farm-land, on which it pastured a large herd of dairy cattle. The company wanted to prove that the fumes from the smelters would not harm dairy cattle, as some farmers claimed. The Aluminum Company plants were nestled among these company farms. Victor's farm was located about two miles west of the Aluminum Company farms.

Victor loved his farm and spent many happy hours puttering around in the yard at his house on the farm. He also loved to talk farming with Dad. Victor felt good when he could help Dad repair machinery. Often he would remind Dad that he had taken a few engineering courses in college. I guess that he liked to think he was able to put his college education to good use. Dad, quite proud himself, did not appreciate Victor's help. At our supper table Dad would make fun of Victor's knowledge of engineering. Still, I do have to say that Dad was always diplomatic with Victor when he offered to help. Dad made Victor think that his assistance was appreciated.

I do not think Dad and Victor ever had an argument. In fact they got along very well. However, as time passed, Dad's respect for Victor's vision for the farm evaporated. For Victor the farm was just a hobby, whereas for Dad the farm was our livelihood. I think the Hultiquists were from wealthy families, and Victor earned a good salary with ALCOA. They had more money than they needed, and they were not interested in running the farm in a way that would make more money. Victor's main interest was in using the farm as a showplace with all the trappings of a working farm, something he could enjoy showing off to his friends and family during weekend visits.

Nineteen forty-three was a good year for crops. The pastures grew, and we needed animals to graze on them. One morning, not long after we moved to the farm, Dad and Victor headed off to the Knoxville cattle market to buy about fifteen head of cattle. Victor had agreed to pay for the cattle and Dad to tend to them. In return Dad would get 15 percent of the profits when Victor sold the cattle.

Dad wanted to buy skinny young yearlings that could be fattened during the summer and then sold in the late fall. But Victor had an entirely different idea. As the cattle came into the ring, Dad would point out the skinny cattle and urge Victor to bid. Victor would say nothing. Then ten beautiful, black Angus cattle, fat as could be, ambled into the bidding ring. Victor became excited and bought all ten. There went Dad's dream of making money on cattle. I remember how discouraged Dad was when he came home that night. He knew that they would not be able to sell the cattle at a profit in the fall.

It was really a shame that Victor did not share Dad's vision. In 1943 the war had pushed the price of beef quite high. If Victor had followed Dad's advice, Dad's earnings from the cattle sales would have greatly increased Dad's earnings for the year. As it turned out, Dad and Victor did not see any profit from the sale of the Angus beef cattle. In fact Victor never intended to sell those Angus cattle at all, and instead he treated them like pets. He kept them to show off to his friends. A few years later, when we left the farm and moved to Mars Hill, Victor still had the same cattle. I guess those cattle were among the luckiest in the world. If Victor had not been in the gallery that day, the cattle would have ended up as hamburgers and steaks. Poor Dad never saw a penny of cattle profits while we lived on the farm.

Well, even if we never earned money from the cattle, we could still receive 25 percent of profits from the produce. The farm was very productive, and we grew a little bit of everything. In fact, as it turned out, we grew too much of everything. We should have focused on one or maybe two crops and made contracts to sell the produce in the local stores. Beans, sweet corn, or both would have been excellent choices. Unfortunately, we had not even heard of a marketing plan, and when spring came around we just planted seeds, and the crops grew and grew, and Mom canned and canned. Victor also canned and canned, and what we could not can Victor gave away. Victor gave away a lot of produce.

I do not think that Victor was interested in selling produce anyway, and poor old Dad didn't know anything about marketing. Dad's marketing strategy was to take a small amount of produce to the area grocery stores in Maryville on Saturday afternoon and try to sell the stuff. We learned that stores hate to buy produce on Saturday afternoon. If the store did buy at that time, then it would have to keep the produce over Sunday when the store was closed. In addition most stores had regular suppliers who kept the store shelves well stocked.

If it was hard enough for us to make ends meet in years we had good crops, the summer of 1944 was unusually tough. The Tennessee River Valley normally received a good amount of rainfall throughout the year. In 1944 the last rain of the spring fell in April, and it did not rain again until August. That summer was unusually hot and dry.

That year we planted our crops, watched them come up, and then we watched the plants in the upper fields shrivel up and die. The crops in the lower fields, those near the lake, survived, but still they didn't produce nearly as much as they would have in a normal year. The only way we could save the season was to replant our crops after the rains had started again in August, far too late to take full advantage of the growing season. The outcome was not good. By the early fall the farm had run out of corn. Lucky for us Victor could use the ALCOA farm produce as his own. Dad and I went down to the ALCOA farm for a wagonload of corn to refill our corncrib.

It was that dismal summer of 1944 that made Dad and Mom realize that we were only getting poorer; we kids were getting older and more expensive, the car needed replacing, and inflation was inching prices up despite the government's price controls. Through all this time Dad's seventy-five-dollar monthly salary remained the same, and with no profit from cattle or produce sales we had to get by with it.

While Victor might have held us back economically, I do have to credit him with saving Dad's life. In late 1944 Dad was thirty-six years old. The invasion of Europe had begun that June, and the war was going pretty well for the

United States, both in Europe and in the Pacific. But this success came at a price as many servicemen were killed or wounded. The Bryson City draft board sent Dad a notice that ordered him to report to Knoxville and go to Atlanta for his physical exam, the first step to induction into the army. Thirty-six is an old age to have to go into the army and take orders from some inexperienced corporal or private first-class. Dad was not too good at taking orders.

We were all upset at the thought of Dad going off to war. We hoped that he would fail the physical and be classified 4F, which meant that you weren't in good enough physical shape to join the army and die in some battle. We thought that he was probably in good health, but we could not be sure. Our only glimmer of hope lay in the fact that the only time any of us had visited a doctor while we were in Tennessee was when Dad had a bad case of the flu, when he decided to quit smoking his hand-rolled Prince Albert Tobacco cigarettes. We did not even see dentists, which would have been pointless for Mom and Dad as they had already had all their teeth pulled and replaced by false teeth. Perversely, we were hoping that, unbeknownst to us, Dad was in horrible condition. But there was not much hope that this would happen. Only real duds were classified 4F. If you could walk, you passed the physical.

After he returned from Atlanta, he complained about all the jerks who were on the bus with him. Dad was pretty dejected. Dad passed the physical exam, just as we had anticipated. All he could see in his future was six weeks of basic training and then being shipped off to fight. We knew that if Dad went to war, chances were that he would not come home. He had no skills, so the army would make him a foot soldier. Foot soldiers never returned.

When Dad told Victor that it looked like he would have to go into the army, Victor said that he would go to Bryson City and try to talk the draft board into giving Dad a permanent deferment. Victor told Dad that if it did not work and Dad had to go to the war, we could live in one of his other houses on the farm until Dad returned. Victor did go to Bryson City, and he did manage to come back with the deferment. I still wonder what kind of lie Victor told the draft board about his farm. I know that his farm was not contributing anything to the war effort. But this did not matter to us. The important thing was that Victor got Dad the deferment.

We had two workhorses, Dan and Jeff. Jeff was a medium-size plain old dumb workhorse. He was always ready to work and never complained. Dan, on the other hand, was a "fancy Dan" breed called the Tennessee Walker. I did not know it at the time, but the Tennessee Walker was developed in the nineteenth century to provide wealthy plantation owners with a comfortable mount from which to oversee work on their land. No one in their right mind would train them to be a workhorse. I think Dan was originally trained to be a riding horse, but somewhere along the line some numbskull tried to train Dan to be a workhorse. No longer good for riding and never good for working, Dan was good for nothing.

I bet that Victor thought he had stumbled on a real two-for-one bargain when he found a horse that appeared to be both a riding horse and a workhorse. Victor might have been fooled, but Dad was not. Dad knew animals; all he had to do was take one look at Dan's fidgety behavior, and he knew we were in for trouble. We were stuck with "Dancing Dan," and like it or not, we had to work the farm with him.

Sometimes Dan was as good a worker as Jeff, but most of the time he just caused havoc. He would work steadily for a few hours, and then, for no apparent reason, he would just stop working and start snorting and dancing. When he started doing this, trying to get him to go back to work was hopeless; nothing we did could get him to start working again. We would slap him with the reins, and he would just stand there, dancing, snorting, and shaking his head with a wild look in his eyes, like he was in a trance. If Dad or I ventured too close to him, he would try to bite us. He was a real devil. This nonsense would continue for at least an hour, and then, again without reason, he would start working again, just like old Jeff.

Dan would act up like this two or three times each week. During the season of heavy work his antics were particularly frustrating because we had to make the most of every day so that we could get all of our work done. I would get so mad at Dan's dancing that I just wanted to kill that useless critter. It made Dad even madder than it would make me, so mad that he would start beating Dan with the reins. I have to say that beating on Dan with those reins did not help. It only made him more stubborn than ever, and this would just make Dad madder and madder. Dad would get so mad and beat old Dan so hard that I would even start feeling sorry for that useless horse. If Dad had had a two-by-four handy during one of these episodes, I'm sure that old Dan would have been long dead.

My worst experience with Dan was in the field along Topton Road, just across from the Robinsons' house. Bobbie, my schoolmate, and her sister were out in the front yard watching us work the field. All at once Dan went into his dancing routine, and no matter how hard we tried, we could not get Dan to work. Dad started cursing and beating him. This battle continued for about two hours while the Robinson kids stood by watching everything. I was so ashamed to have my friends see Dad behave like this. But even I was not reckless enough to try to calm down a madman who was facing down a mad horse. After a while Dad got so tired from beating Dan that he had to sit down and rest in the shade of a tree. A few minutes later Dan calmed down and went back to work.

I have always tried to figure out why that horse was so ornery. I find it hard to believe that it was just because he wasn't the right breed to be a workhorse. I think that he must have had some type of mental condition, just as some people do. When I think about this from Dan's perspective, I would guess that old Dan was just as confounded by Dad and me as we were by him. He probably spent a lot of time trying to figure out why we were always so ornery. I will say that Dad never quit trying to win Dan over. One day he even went so far as to play cowboy and ride Dan to one of the far pastures to bring the cows in for milking. Dan danced around while Dad saddled him. Then Dad mounted him and took off at a gallop across the field. On the way they came to a small gully that Dad had decided Dan could easily jump, so Dad sped up as he approached the gully. But that old stubborn horse stopped dead in his tracks, and poor old Dad tumbled over the horse's head. Bruised and angry, Dad got up, led Dan back to the barn, and put him in his stall. Dad never tried to play cowboy again. He just added this episode to his list of reasons why he hated Dan.

Dad continually complained to Victor about Dan, but it took a couple of years for Victor to notice. Finally Victor relented and agreed to buy another workhorse. Dad and I were pleasantly surprised when Victor arrived on the farm with one fine workhorse. Major, the new horse, was a big black monster. He weighed about one thousand pounds, but he was as gentle as a cow. All he wanted to do was work and eat. The first workday after he arrived we hitched Major and Jeff to the wagon and headed for the fields and watched in awe as Major and Jeff plowed as a team. It was a joy to behold. When Dad said "get up," Major moved out smartly, and I suppose Jeff was surprised and moved out immediately as well. Jeff fell right into step with Major, and I would imagine that he enjoyed working alongside a real workhorse. Having peace between Dad and the horses not only made us happy; it also made us more productive. I suppose old Dan was happier too because Dad took him to the pasture and let him stay there where he could dance to his heart's content.

The horses did not have to work when we were hoeing. On these days Dad and I would put the horses out to pasture in the early morning. Then we would put our hoes over our shoulders and head for the fields. A weed called Johnson grass infested most of east Tennessee. Johnson grass grows about three inches a day, and the root system spreads at about the same rate. Cultivating between the cornrows with a four- or five-tined plow would not stop the grass from growing. In fact when we used the cultivator to plow, it just seemed to make the Johnson grass grow faster. The only way to keep the grass under control, until the corn was tall enough to fend for itself, was to take a hoe to the Johnson grass. The grass grew in small patches, so controlling the weed, although difficult, was not impossible.

One day after a hard day hoeing the fields without the horses, Dad and I went to the barn to do some chores. As usual the horses were at the gate, anxiously and impatiently waiting to be fed. Major was standing with his head over the gate, Jeff was at his side, and Dan, as usual, was dancing around being a real pest. Then Dan made the mistake of taking a nip at Major's backside, and old Major got fed up and hauled off and kicked Dan with his big eight-inch hoof. It was a perfect shot. The kick landed right on one of Dan's lower front legs and snapped it like a twig. I guess old Dan was more surprised than anyone when he could not dance anymore.

Dad headed down to Victor's house, where he found Victor puttering around in his rock garden. Dad told Victor about Dan's broken leg, and Victor went into his house and came back with his pistol. He and Dad then went to the gate where old Dan was standing on three legs, dangling his shattered front leg in the air. Dad took the pistol and crawled over the gate. He walked over to Dan and, with a slight smile on his face, carefully aimed the pistol at Dan's head and pulled the trigger. Old Dan fell to the ground, deader than a doornail. Dad handed the pistol back to Victor and told Victor that that he would bury Dan. Peace prevailed the next year. When the war ended, Victor bought a brand-new Ford tractor with all the tools, and Dad let the horses stay in the pasture.

Overall I enjoyed the farm. We all did a lot of work, but there also was plenty of time to roam about the farm and along the cliffs above the river. Mom and Dad let me go hunting alone, an activity I particularly enjoyed. Victor loaned me a 28-gauge shotgun to keep the crows out of the cornfields. I liked to hide in the cornfield and wait for the crows. The crows would fly into the cornfield, settle on the ears, and start eating away. It did not take long for me to learn that crows are crafty birds. A sharp-eyed crow would always be perched in a nearby tree as a lookout. I would try my best to quietly creep to the area where the crows were feeding, but the lookout would always see me and sound the alarm before I could even get off one shot. I would take a couple of shots as the crows flew away, but I never hit a one.

Sometimes I went rabbit hunting with my faithful dog. Fido and I would thrash along through the bushes in the pasture, trying to jump a rabbit. When we were lucky enough to jump a rabbit, Fido would take off after him. When a rabbit is chased by a dog, it will circle around and return to its nesting area. So I would stay put, waiting for Fido to chase the rabbit back to where I was standing. But Fido was a large, short-legged dog and could not run very fast, so a rabbit did not have to run far to get away from him. The rabbit would soon be out of sight, at which point a good hunting dog would trail a rabbit by smelling its tracks. Fido would never do this. Instead he would give up the chase and come sit by me. I think that maybe Fido could not smell well enough to track a rabbit. But then again I know that he did a pretty good job smelling food. I finally decided that he was just plain lazy. I never managed to kill a rabbit that Fido had chased. At night I would take Fido out opossum and fox hunting. I used traps, and I did catch a few opossums, but never a fox.

Victor had a slim, long-legged, and jumpy dog named Smoky. It did not take long for Victor to tire of Smoky, and he gave him to us. I think Victor wanted to get rid of Smoky because he was useless at hunting; he was even more useless than Fido.

One day Sibbald, Don, and I were out playing with Fido and Smoky down by the lake when suddenly Smoky took a nip at Don. In the blink of an eye Fido jumped on Smoky. Fido beat the socks off Smoky, and throughout that afternoon Smoky kept well away from Don and Fido. As far as we were concerned, on that day Fido was not a useless, short-legged hunting dog—he was a hero.

That evening we told Dad what had happened, and Dad told us that he did not cotton to a biting dog. Dad did not waste time thinking about what to do. He simply got his shotgun, went out in the yard, and called Smoky. Fido and Smoky bounded over to him just as friendly as could be. Dad started walking toward the barn, and the dogs followed. Then Dad went on past the barn up to the top of the ridge. We heard a shot. Then Dad and Fido came back down to the house.

Most winters in the Tennessee River Valley are mild and wet with short cold spells. The pastures remain green and continue to grow through the winter and are ready to mow at the first sign of spring. The cattle could almost last the winter without eating any cut hay. For us this meant that in most years we could accumulate quite a bit of cut hay. Nineteen forty-five was one such year, and by the fall the barn loft was so full of hay that we had to start stacking it in the fields.

To take care of the hay, Victor borrowed a motorized hay baler from the ALCOA farm. The day he arrived with the baler, Victor announced that starting the next night he and his son Charles would come, and all of us would work every evening until ten o'clock until we had baled all the hay. The next four days we worked until all the hay was baled and stored in the barn loft.

The evenings were hot and humid, and the hay was dusty and scratchy. I got hot, dirty, and itchy. Moreover, I got pissed off that all this work was making me miss all my evening radio programs. Toward the end of the project I was tired, and while everyone else continued to work, I would stop and rest quite often. Each time I stopped, Charles or Victor would be right there telling me to get off my lazy butt and get back to work. This was my first experience with a straw boss. I was even more pissed off when I found out that Victor did not plan to pay us for this extra work. Dad and I were nothing but slave labor in this nighttime hay-baling operation.

I usually worked on the farm with Dad, but Victor never paid me for this work. Sometimes he would pay me for other work, but when it came to the farm Victor considered our whole family to be his farmhands, and we were all supposed to work alongside Victor and Dad. He expected all this labor for a measly seventy-five dollars a month. The only thing that he would do for us was that occasionally he would bring an old black man from Alcoa to help when we could not keep up with the work.

I suppose that I should have been happy that Victor would pay me twenty-five cents each time I mowed his lawn, which I usually did once a week during the spring and summer. I did this with a push mower, and it took about four hours, and under the hot sun it was very hard work. Whenever he paid me, he would complain that I had not pulled up all the dandelions, and he was right. This was something

that I was not about to do. By midsummer the lawn was
nothing but a field of dandelions. I would take his lip, say
nothing, and pocket his quarter.

During the summer I would also herd Victor's prized
cattle. By early summer the grass along the farm road edges
would be growing like mad, and I would watch the cattle
for a few hours each morning as they grazed on this choice
grass. For this job he paid me a measly five cents an hour.

In the summer of 1947, when I was fifteen, Victor hired
me to clear the pasture on the mountainside west of his
house. He promised to pay me twenty-five cents an hour.
He wanted the area cleared of all brush, bushes, weeds,
and briars. He also wanted a large area north of a small
grove of trees supporting muscatel-type grapes cleared of
all the small pine trees. The pine trees were about fifteen
feet tall, and the area where the pine trees grew was nothing but a red clay gully.

I had learned a lot about erosion in school, and I decided to show off what I had learned. In my classes I had
learned that the pine trees provided good protection from
erosion. I told Dad and Victor that I thought the pine trees
should remain so as to control erosion and protect the hillside. Dad and Victor were not impressed. They ordered me
to cut the pine trees down.

Well, I ended up doing that miserable job. When I say
miserable, I mean miserable. The weather was hot and humid, and I would become sweaty, itchy, and tired. Worst
of all, neither Victor nor Dad was satisfied with my work,
no matter how hard I tried. Never in a single day did I do

as much work as they thought I should have done. I have to admit that I did not try very hard.

Every evening Dad would talk to me about how I had to work harder and quit being so lazy. I guess Dad wanted to be proud of my work in front of Victor, and I admit that I didn't give him any reason to be proud. As for me, I kept it clear in my mind that I was working for Victor and not Dad. Whenever Dad criticized me, I refused to listen to or answer him. I simply put what he said out of my mind.

A couple times a week Victor would come to the pasture and berate me for not working faster. He would point out that at the rate I was working, it would take me all summer to complete the job. Each time he said this, I would assure Victor that indeed I would take that long and that I would be done by the time school started. I just kept taking his scolding, working on my schedule, and collecting my ten dollars at the end of each week.

I finished the job just before school started, as I had planned. I also cut down those beautiful pine trees, just as Dad and Victor had ordered me to do. I placed the cut trees in the gullies in the hope that this would stall the erosion until new trees started growing. That was the last big job that I would do for Victor.

Dad and I were not getting along too well that year, particularly when it came to work. We had one of our worst conflicts that year when he decided that he and I should cut firewood with a two-man crosscut saw. He would take one end of the saw and I the other. Because I had short arms, I had to bend the saw when my arms extended fully to the rear. When the saw bent, it would not travel smoothly through the log. Each stroke was awkward, which would make Dad fume. At times I imagined that I was that old horse, Dancing Dan, and I realized how Dan must have felt when Dad got mad at him. After cutting wood with Dad a few times, I decided that it would be better to cut all the firewood myself rather than listen to Dad grumble. I guess Dad was smart to have figured out how to get me to cut all the firewood.

With the help of our horse Jeff I managed to complete the job. I would go to the woods, cut down a big tree, and trim it. Then I would have Jeff pull the tree to the wood-pile in the yard. Then I would cut the tree into firewood all by myself with the two-man crosscut saw. The sawing took longer, but it was so much more peaceful.

I think that our conflicts around work had to do with the fact that I was fifteen, and Dad thought that I should be doing the work of a man. I guess that he thought that he was preparing me to follow in his footsteps, that he was training me to be a manual laborer. Well, the experience of working for Dad and Victor on the farm sure did make me think about what I wanted to do with my life, and I was sure that farming was out of the question. I thought that driving a truck might be a good job.

Before Dad accepted the offer to work on the Hultiquist farm, he had considered taking a job on the Spence farm: a farm that was nestled on a wide bend in the Tennessee River, about two miles downstream from Victor's. It was a large farm, more than two thousand acres, that produced large amounts of chickens, eggs, cattle, milk, and produce. About fifteen tenant families lived and worked on the farm. After he had decided on the Hultiquist offer, Dad told Grandpa Smith about the opening on the Spence farm. Grandpa Smith took the job, and he and his family joined us in Tennessee.

Grandpa found himself tending two chicken houses, each with two hundred hens. Grandpa was not a hard or steady worker when he was in Cherokee, and his habits did not change after he moved to Tennessee. His kids ended up doing most of the work, and Grandpa Smith had barely been working there for a year when he was fired. From there Grandpa moved his family to a dairy farm across the river from the Spence farm. He did no better at this job, and once again he made his children do all the work. He lived there for a while, but eventually he quit, gave up farming in Tennessee, and moved back to Cherokee.

When Grandpa moved to Tennessee, he made the mistake of selling his place on Kate Lambert Branch. Mom and Dad knew that he would not have anywhere to live after he moved back to Cherokee, so they let Grandpa and his family move into our house in the cove. Shortly after that Grandpa purchased our old house on the road and moved there with his family. I would guess that he didn't pay much for the place: I know for a fact that he didn't have much money. That's where Grandpa Smith and his family lived until Grandpa died of prostate cancer in 1948. Estaline, his second wife, and their children continued to live there until the mid-1950s. The house remained in the Smith family until the late 1990s, when my uncle Jarrett died.

By 1943 Grandma Lambert's tuberculosis had become worse. About once a week Dad and I would walk to Mentor, where Dad would call his brother Gillian, the Cherokee telephone operator, to find out how Grandma was doing. Each time Gillian would tell Dad that Grandma's condition had worsened. This really got to Dad. He was close to Grandma, and here he was in Tennessee, and he could not even talk with her on the telephone.

By the summer of 1943 Dad and Mom had saved enough money for Dad to take his one-week vacation and go to Cherokee to see Grandma. He was also planning to take advantage of this trip to replace the tires on our car and bring it back to Tennessee. Victor, who according to the government was a farmer, was kind enough to claim that he needed the tires for the farm. The government let him get four new tires for our old 1934 Chevy.

We made our plans for the trip. Victor said that he and Mrs. Hultquist would pick us up early on the first Sunday in August and take us and our new tires to Cherokee. It turned out that that would be too late, and poor old Dad did not get to see Grandma. On that very Sunday at two in the morning a Maryville sheriff's deputy came to our door and told Dad that the sheriff's office in Maryville had received word from Gillian that Grandma Lambert had died on Saturday afternoon. Dad was in shock. I felt sorry for him. He was just one day short of seeing her. She was only fifty-four.

Victor dropped us off at Grandma's house before noon. Gillian, who also took her death hard, told us that Grandma had been sitting on the porch on Saturday afternoon and was very excited about our visit. Out of nowhere she had a seizure and died at about three in the afternoon.

We went into the living room, where many of Grandma's friends were sitting. Grandma had been prepared for burial and was laid out on her bed with a silver dollar on each of her eyes. I am sure someone took the silver dollars before they buried her. About thirty minutes after dropping us off, Victor drove back into the yard and asked for Dad. Victor told Dad that he had forgotten to pay him his July salary, and he wanted to know if Dad needed any money. Dad said that we had enough money to get back to the farm and Victor could pay him then. Everyone who heard the conversation told Dad that he was very lucky to have such a good boss. Despite my misgivings about Victor, when I think back to those times now, I have to agree.

Grandma was buried in the Birdtown cemetery that Sunday afternoon. The next day we went to the cove and replaced the tires on the car. We stayed with Aunt Grace and Uncle Neal for the rest of the week, as we did on our other vacations from Tennessee. When we got ready to return to the farm, Grace and Neal gave us Fido, the mongrel dog I mentioned earlier. Dad put Fido in a pasteboard box and tied the box onto the running board of the car for the trip back to Tennessee. Old Fido served as my companion and Dad's loyal hunting dog until he had to be shot in 1959.

We drove back to the farm in our car in August 1943, and our life changed almost immediately. We started going shopping and selling small amounts of produce in Maryville almost every Saturday afternoon. After a while we even started going to the theater for the Saturday-afternoon Western movies. This quickly became a regular event because the theater showed a serial movie. Each Saturday the movie ended with the hero facing certain death, and we had to see the next installment to find out if the hero lived or died.

Dad was brave but somewhat dishonest when he bought our tickets. He paid for adult tickets for himself and Mom and kiddy tickets for us children, even though some of us were older than twelve. One day the ticket taker called Dad on it and made him buy the adult tickets for us older kids. We never went to the movies again.

Our lives would change again in 1943, when Victor pulled some strings and had the Rural Electric Administration install a power line to our houses. They wired our house with an outlet and an overhead hanging cord light in each room. Victor pulled some more strings, and Dad purchased a Norge refrigerator, and we discarded our icebox. It was hard to believe how good cold milk and butter tasted. Mom started making ice cream for dessert as well as one of my favorites, Jell-O. We bought an electric radio, and Victor gave us an electric alarm clock. Each morning at quarter past five that darn clock rang—ding, ding, ding, ding, ding,

ding. We could hear the dinging all over the house. Eventually Dad would get up and turn off the alarm.

Even when we were in Tennessee we never socialized unless it was with kin. When Grandpa Smith lived in Tennessee, we visited his family often. When they left and moved back to Cherokee, we didn't visit anyone. We passed our Sunday afternoons tossing horseshoes, and sometimes we played rook. We also did a lot of fishing, both as a pastime and for food. Our catch included carp, bream, catfish, and a few bass. Knoxville and other cities and towns upstream dumped raw sewage into the river and polluted our lake, but no one, much less us, seemed to mind.

Dad was an impatient fisherman. As soon as he tossed his line into the water, he wanted a big fish to be on the end of it. He was not interested in the six- or eight-inch fish we usually caught; he really wanted to catch big fish and a lot of them. To improve his catch he built a fish trap, not unlike a child's minnow trap. It was about three by three feet and six feet long. He made the frame with two-by-fours and then covered the frame with chicken wire. Each end of the trap had a chicken-wire cone protruding into the trap that allowed the fish to swim in but made it difficult for them to find their way out. It mattered little to Dad that fish traps were illegal in Tennessee.

When Dad completed the trap, he hung part of a chicken carcass in the center of the trap. Then he and I waited until night to carry the trap to the lake. We loaded the trap onto our flat-bottom boat and quietly slipped out to the center of the lake. We tied a couple of large rocks to the trap to make sure that it would sink. Then we slid the trap over the edge of the boat, paddled back to shore, and tied off the tag line. With this work complete we went to bed.

The next morning Dad went out to the back porch to wash up. As he looked down toward the lake, he noticed that one corner of the fish trap was sticking out of the water. He rushed into our bedroom and told me to get up and dressed and to follow him. We ran to the boat and paddled as quickly as we could out to the trap. We found a large dead turtle trapped in the corner of the trap. The turtle had gone into the trap and drowned. Dad cut the wire and let the turtle float away, and we held the trap just under water while we paddled to the shore. We made sure that no one was watching, and then we pulled the trap out of the water, carried it to the house, and hid it in some bushes. The trap also contained a twenty-four-inch bass that we ate that night for supper. From that time forward Dad stuck to legal fishing.

Once Victor asked Dad if he would like to go fox hunting with Victor and some of his friends. Thinking himself a keen hunter, Dad accepted the offer. Saturday night came, and Dad took his shotgun and headed up to Victor's house.

The next morning at breakfast, after Dad had returned, I could see that he was disgusted. He explained that he got up to Victor's house and found Victor and six of his friends ready to go. Dad said the men had six or seven of the best-looking hunting dogs he had ever seen and that he was excited that he would have the chance to hunt with them.

Then they told Dad he would not need his gun, so he left it at Victor's house. He said that shortly after dark they went to the top of the mountain that overlooked the river and built a big fire and then turned the dogs loose. Then they all sat on a couple of logs near the fire and passed their time smoking cigars. After a while they heard the dogs barking, and everyone got excited. One man would say, "That's old Red," and another would say, "That's old Blue."

Dad said this stupidity lasted about four hours. All they did was sit there and listen to their dogs bark. Finally, one of the men started calling the dogs. The dogs came back, and the owners collared and leashed them. When all the dogs were accounted for, the group went back down to Victor's house, where Dad got his gun and came home. Dad said he would never go fox hunting with Victor again. He said it was the stupidest hunting trip he had ever been on.

We did not go to church regularly until Ballard's Chapel, located on Topton Road, about five miles up toward Knoxville, started running a bus each Sunday morning to pick people up. Even then at first Mom and Dad did not go, but they did send us older kids. I suppose they just wanted us out of their sight for a while each week, and church offered a perfect opportunity. Eventually, Dad decided one summer that we were going to get religion. The Church of God had a "Tabernacle" on Topton Road. That year we went to the revival almost every night.

After we had attended a few services, Dad decided that it was time for us to be saved. That night the sermon seemed to last forever. About halfway through the invitation song someone came and asked if we wanted to be saved. Dad rose and followed him to the altar. The rest of us tagged along after Dad. When we reached the altar rail, we knelt down and closed our eyes.

I knew that I was supposed to keep my eyes closed, but I did peek out now and then to see what was going on and how everybody was faring. Soon after we arrived at the altar, three or four people started praying over us. After fifteen minutes of this praying Dad and the rest of the family were bawling their eyes out. This is what you were supposed to do when you were saved. The shame of your past sins was supposed to make you cry. But try as I did, I could not cry. I couldn't shed one tear no matter how hard I tried, and I sure did try hard, and this made me very upset. Mountain people said that if a person could not cry when they were saved, they were not ashamed of their sins and therefore they were in the hands of the devil and their situation was hopeless.

It rather scared me to think that I could not be saved, so I did the only thing I could do: I pretended to cry, and I did a poor job at it. I wondered if my brothers and sisters, especially Betty and Helen, were also faking it. When I peeked out, I realized that if they were faking it, they were doing a much better job than I was. We all "cried" for several minutes, and then, following Dad's lead, we rose up from our knees, and the preacher declared that we had been saved. I sure was glad that ordeal was over.

Once we were saved our evenings changed. Rather than sitting around listening to the radio, as we had always done, Dad started reading the Bible to us. He started with Genesis and read right though to Revelations. Each evening he would read for about an hour, and then he would say a prayer before he put us to bed. Dad could really pray a good prayer. They would last a good quarter hour, and he left nothing out. He thanked God for just about everything and asked him to bless and take care of about everybody and everything. I hated this evening devotion. It interfered with my evening radio programs, which began at about the same time as Dad's Bible readings. And no matter how much I tried to get out of it, Dad would hear nothing of my complaints.

I don't think the Bible readings did much good anyway. We children understood absolutely nothing of what Dad read to us, and I do not think Dad understood much more than we did. Poor Dad also had to skip many of the readings because he could not pronounce the big words. Then there were the parts about sex, drunkenness, and other bad things. He started skipping those parts too. These things embarrassed Dad, and he thought it was wrong to expose us children to this stuff, even though it was in the Bible. As for me I was glad that he skipped over these parts. The readings went much faster.

I would get so tired and bored during these Bible readings, and this would just make me feel guilty. I felt like the devil really had a firm hold on me and would never let go. Each night I was so glad when Dad said, "Amen" and, after a brief moment, I was free to listen to the radio. Dad eventually made it through the last chapter of the Bible, marking the end of our family devotions. I think Dad was almost as happy as I was that it was finally over.

During the war the government pursued a number of policies to keep the economy stable. The government issued ration books to control how much of an item a family could buy. We never used all of our stamps, so we gave our extra ones to Victor. The government also placed price controls on just about everything. Merchants who violated the controls were fined and sometimes sentenced to jail. These unscrupulous merchants would also face the humiliation of being labeled unpatriotic. The system seemed to work well for perishable goods that were in short supply, such as food and gasoline. But they were less effective for durable goods, and many merchants found ways to work around them.

In the waning days of the war Dad decided to buy a car. He found a nice 1942 Plymouth on a lot in Maryville. He asked the salesman how much the car would cost. The salesman, thinking that Dad could not afford the car, told him that the price was around eight hundred dollars. Dad figured that he could handle the payments, and he told the salesman that he was interested. The salesman then explained that the government had set the price and that the dealer would provide financing that Dad could pay off with monthly payments. Then the salesman added that the dealer would have to have another eight hundred dollars paid in cash before Dad could drive the car off the lot. The salesman added that no record would be made of this cash payment. At this point Dad decided that he could not afford the car. Those who had money went along with this business practice. Poor old Dad just did not have the money to take part in this kind of business.

This was too bad, because our old Chevrolet was about to die. Unable to afford the Plymouth, we had to find a way to make the Chevrolet roadworthy. The biggest problem was that the car needed a new engine block. Dad and I removed the engine from the car and took the worn engine block to Knoxville, where we traded it for ninety-seven dollars and bought a rebuilt engine block. Dad also ordered a new muffler from Sears.

When we arrived back on the farm, we replaced the engine block and got ready for a test ride. When we started the new engine, the engine ran roughly for about five minutes, and then the bearings seized. So we took out the engine again, and Dad sent the block back to the shop to have the bearings replaced. The block was still under warranty, so the shop replaced the bearings for free, even though the failure was clearly our fault. By late that evening we had installed the new block.

The next morning Dad decided to drive us kids up to the Rowlands' house, where the school bus would pick us up. I tried to talk Dad into letting us walk, as we had always done, but he would have nothing of it. He tried, unsuccessfully, to start the engine so many times that the battery discharged. Again I told Dad that we would walk up to the bus stop. Again he refused to hear anything of it. He was determined to take us in his refurbished car. We kids just stood there watching Dad trying to start the car. Our waiting and watching only made Dad even more determined.

After the battery died, Dad decided to have one of the horses pull the car to the top of the hill and then let the car roll down the hill, at which time he would put the car in gear, let out the clutch, and turn the engine over. By then we had already missed our bus, so I gave up trying to convince him to let us walk to school and began to help him.

The horse pulled the car to the top of the hill, and Dad turned the car around. He got in and let the car roll down the hill. The hill was steep, and the car picked up a lot of speed. With the car going full speed, Dad let out the clutch. The engine caught and backfired explosively, and a plume of blue smoke trailed from underneath the car as it sped down the hill past our house with Dad at the wheel. The engine did not start. Dad stopped the car and got out. The odor from the exhaust was strong. Dad and I got down on our hands and knees and looked under the car, where we saw our brand-new Sears muffler split wide open. I went up the hill and got the horse, and we pulled the car back to our yard. Then Dad let us kids walk to school.

We were very late, but the teachers listened to our story and then told us to take our seats and not to worry about it. By the time we got home that evening, Dad had already removed the muffler, packed it up, and sent it back to Sears. A few days later we received a brand-new muffler that Dad installed. This time Dad had a mechanic check out the engine. The mechanic found that Dad had connected the spark plugs in the wrong firing order. The mechanic made adjustments and then started the engine. This time the engine ran like a new watch. The old Chevy was now running well, but it still had the problems of an old car. The steering gear was worn, and the fabric roof leaked like a sieve.

One afternoon in the spring of 1944 or 1945 Phillip drove his big log truck into our yard. Gillian hopped out of the cab, grabbed his suitcase from the truckbed, and announced that he had come to stay. Without pausing to think about it, Mom and Dad moved out of their bedroom and let Gillian have their bed. He would stay for a long six long months.

Over dinner a few days later Mom let slip that she had written to Grandpa Smith and told him that Gillian had come to stay with us. Boy, did Gillian hit the roof. He made it clear to all of us that he did not want anyone in Cherokee to know where he was. I immediately knew that whatever Gillian had done to bring him to our home, it must have been bad. Later I would hear rumors that he had been bootlegging and running a brothel out of Grandma's house. I also heard that he had stolen money from the tribal office. Gillian was not known to be the most honest person. I could tell that he sure was living up to his reputation.

Gillian asserted that Mom had to go to Cherokee and get the letter before Grandpa had a chance to read it. I could not believe that he would talk to my mom like that. I was even more shocked when I looked down the table and saw Dad just sitting there nodding in agreement. Even Mom just sat there quietly.

The next day Mom did exactly what Gillian wanted her to do. Dad took Mom to the highway, where she caught the bus to Knoxville. From there she caught the bus to Cherokee. Mom managed to arrive before the letter. When the letter arrived, she took it and burned it before Grandpa even knew it was there. To be honest, I don't think it did any good. Grandpa was no dummy, even though he acted like one at times. I am sure he knew exactly what had been going on at Gillian's house. After all he lived only a stone's throw up the road. Grandpa also had to have known that Gillian had disappeared and that he had to be at our house in Tennessee. Still, Grandpa never bothered to ask Mom about Gillian or his whereabouts while she was there.

Years later I asked my Mom about this episode, and she denied that it had ever happened. But I know that it did, and to this day it has puzzled me. Why were Mom and Dad so willing to answer to Gillian's demands? I can only conclude that there was something fishy about Mom and Dad's relationship with Gillian. I sometimes wonder if he knew that Mom was already pregnant with me when she and Dad married and they were afraid that he would tell us kids. I know that they wanted this to remain a secret because they kept it from us for fifty years. We would not learn the truth until my sister Helen would go down to the Sylva courthouse to find out the date of their marriage so that we could plan their fiftieth wedding anniversary. She learned that they married on December 24, 1931, six months before I was born.

Gillian settled in, and Mom and Dad catered to him like slaves. At Dad's urging Victor, good man that he was, gave Gillian a job that paid eleven dollars a week. Gillian, cad that he was, just put the money in his pocket and never offered Mom and Dad anything for room and board. He just acted like it was his due.

Although she would not say anything to him directly, I know that Mom did not like having Gillian around. When Mom and I were working in the garden or when Mom was washing on the scrub board, she complained about Gillian. She said that she quit having children because she felt that she could not give another child the care it would have needed. She once told me that Gillian required more work than it took to care for the whole family. The day she told me that, Mom was especially mad because she was washing his clothes.

Fortunately for everyone, Gillian got up one morning, ate breakfast, packed his suitcase, and said he was leaving. Dad tried to convince him to stay. Gillian had six months of savings he had earned working on the farm, and I think Dad knew that Gillian was up to no good. I am sure that he thought that Gillian was on his way to Knoxville to gamble and drink his money away. But Gillian insisted that he had to go, and Dad finally agreed to take him to catch the bus to Knoxville. While it was fun to have Gillian around, and we spent a lot of time working and fishing together, I was glad he was gone, and I hoped that he would never return.

When he left the farm, he went straight to Knoxville, met up with some of his friends, and passed a couple of months gambling, drinking, and chasing women. Then he returned to our house without a cent to his name. He just showed up without notice, just like he had done the first time. And he moved right back into Mom and Dad's bedroom without even saying thank you.

During this visit he worked in the town of Alcoa and helped Charles Hultiquist, Victor's son, build an apartment house. Charles paid him the same weekly salary of eleven dollars. I suppose this time Gillian was too ashamed to take free room and board, and he said he was going to pay Mom eleven dollars a month. Mom gladly took the money, and she did not complain as much this time since he was paying for his keep. This time he stayed about six months, and then one morning, just like before, he got up, took his money, and left.

Despite his antics I felt close to Gillian. He was pleasant and kind to me—a real pal. As I grew older, I came to realize that he was never anything more than a no-good bum. He was an alcoholic, not the kind who drank all the time, but rather the type who drank now and then and would go on long binges. The last time I saw him was when my wife and I were living in Calderwood. One Sunday afternoon Dad and I went to see him at his apartment in Knoxville, where we found him alone and drunk, lazing around in his underwear.

He let us into the apartment, and then he went straight into his bedroom and stood in the middle of the bed, jumping up and down like a three-year-old. He had a bottle of bourbon in his right hand, and he was ranting and raving. Dad tried to reason with him. I said something that pissed him off even more, and he called me a little son-of-a-bitch. He also said that no one in the family cared anything about him. I think he was right about that.

This was not a pretty sight for Dad, and I really felt sorry for him. I just stood there looking at Gillian and thinking, "What a fool." I said nothing more, and Dad stopped trying to talk with him. I was proud of Dad. I know it must have hurt Dad to see his brother acting like the drunken bum that he was. We left and went back to the car. As we left the apartment, Gillian was still carrying on like a brat.

While he was in Knoxville, Gillian started living with a cafe employee named Hazel. Gillian and Hazel lived in Knoxville until the early 1960s, when they moved to the Cherokee area and lived in a dilapidated trailer in Ela, a small community between Cherokee and Bryson City. By then Mom and Dad had already returned to the reservation and built a restaurant on Soco Road.

Mom and Dad tried running the restaurant for a while but finally gave up and leased it to a Swedish man whom they called, quite simply, "the Swede." He lived in the same trailer park as Hazel and Gillian, and it wasn't long before Hazel and the Swede were involved. Needless to say, Gillian was drinking more than ever.

Gillian owned an old Nash automobile. One night around

1966 Gillian, drunk as a skunk, allegedly ran a hose from the exhaust pipe to the front seat and then crawled into the car and started the engine. The Swain County sheriff thought that Gillian's death was suspicious because Gillian was too drunk to have rigged up the exhaust pipe by himself. After that Hazel and the Swede disappeared, and no one ever heard from them again.

Other relatives stayed with us while we were in Tennessee. When Mom's youngest sister, Phoebe, took a job at the Oak Ridge Uranium Plant, she decided it would be best to leave her two toddlers, Eugene and David, with us. Now and then she would visit the farm and spend some time with her children.

A while later she quit her job, married Thurman Schuler, retrieved her children, and they all moved into a miserable Knoxville slum. Not too long after that Thurman died of tuberculosis, and around 1950 Phoebe would find her way out of the slum. The Public Housing Authority approved her application for a nice duplex in a Knoxville housing project, where she met a building maintenance worker at the project named Fred. When I met him in 1951, I thought he was one impressive man. He was slim, handsome, and he drove with unmistakable pride a big black 1949 Oldsmobile. Later they would move to Mars Hill, where Fred worked with Dad in the maintenance crew. After working for a while at that job, he returned to Knoxville and started a successful contracting business in housing maintenance and remodeling for Sears.

After Fred retired, he and Phoebe moved to Soco, where they lived near Mom and Dad. It was there that I came across Fred again, and this time I was not impressed. Fred had aged into an old fat man who was always chewing tobacco, which he spit into his constant companion, a tin can.

Among our other guests were Aunt Grace and Uncle Neal, who came to see us from Cherokee a couple of times. Once they came with Grace's daughter by her first husband and her daughter's husband. I never liked Grace's son-in-law. As far as I know, he never had a job. When my cousin married him, I decided that I never did like her much either. In their own way I thought that they made a very good match.

The young couple slept in Mom and Dad's bedroom during their visit. This is where my sister Helen kept her money jar, which held her life savings of about seven dollars. After they all went home, Helen went into the bedroom to count her money, only to find the jar empty. We set ourselves to trying to figure out where the money had gone. It was beyond us to believe that Grace or Neal would steal money from a child. We weren't sure about my cousin, but we decided that we should give her the benefit of the doubt. However, when we pondered the question as to whether her husband would steal, our answer was "Yes," and we pronounced him guilty.

Although we were convinced that he took the money, we never did anything about it. We knew that we could not prove it. We never even said anything to any of them about the empty jar because we were afraid of ruining our delightful relationship with Aunt Grace and Uncle Neal. When I think about it, every year we would go to Cherokee and spend a week with Grace and Neal. If they or their children took the money, I guess we owed it to them for their hospitality anyway.

Mentor School

Mentor School was a poor country school on the road to the airport about one and a half miles from our home. It was one of those traditional schools where each morning before class the teachers read a Bible passage and then sang a couple of songs. One of these songs was always the Tennessee state song, which made an impression on me, and even today, more than fifty years later, I can hum the tune. When I was a kid I thought that the song was really great. Now I think it is corny, and I wonder if the song is still the state song.

The school building was simple. Coal-burning stoves heated the schoolrooms in winter, and open windows cooled them in the spring and fall, not that this made the rooms any more comfortable. The kitchen and lunchroom were downstairs in a half basement. The girls had an outdoor privy behind the school on the edge of the playground, and our privy was a little farther from the school building, down by the red clay basketball court. We also had a softball diamond, and the rest of the school grounds were playgrounds.

The school went from first through eighth grades but only had four classrooms. This meant that each teacher taught at least two grades in each room, an arrangement that suited me well. While my teacher was teaching the grade on the other side of the room, I could do my homework or I could follow the lesson that the teacher was presenting to the other grade. This arrangement gave me time to catch up on all I had not learned while I was in the Cherokee school.

We children dreaded going to a white school. In Birdtown everyone told us that Indian schools were not as good as and much easier than white schools. Before my first day at Mentor School was over, I knew that the rumors we had heard in Birdtown were true.

I entered Mentor School in fourth grade, Betty in third, and Helen in second, the same grades as we were in at Birdtown. We should have done as Grandpa Smith's kids had done and dropped back a year. But I was already old for my grade, and I did not want to drop back and be even older than my classmates. Because of this I found myself at the bottom of my class. At Birdtown fourth-graders were still printing. At Mentor fourth-grade students were expected to know how to write cursive, something I had to quickly teach myself to do if I were to have any chance to keep up with the other kids. Miss Johnnie, my fourth-grade teacher, seemed to understand that I was far behind and trying my best to catch up. She was very patient and never pushed me too hard.

Math came to me easily, so it was not hard for me to catch up with the other students in that subject. English, however, was a different matter. It felt as though the Cherokee school had taught me nothing about reading and writing. I managed to improve my reading ability because our reader had interesting stories about all sorts of topics, such as the jungles of Africa. This really motivated me to catch up with the other students, which I did. But catching up in writing proved much more of a challenge.

About once a week Miss Johnnie had us write a paragraph about our reading assignment. The first time I received this assignment, I panicked. I didn't even know what a paragraph was. Nor was I brave enough to ask the teacher. I managed to muster the courage to ask one of my playmates at recess. Boy, did he laugh. I just took his abuse quietly, and in turn he patiently explained the meaning of the word "paragraph." I learned that knowing what a paragraph was did not make it any easier to write one. No matter how many times I read a story, my mind could not find words to put on the paper that lay in front of me. The words would not come. While that year was hard, I hung in there, and with Miss Johnnie's help, before long I was writing paragraphs like all the other students. Miss Johnnie generously gave me straight Es for excellent on my report card, even though I knew I did not earn them. At the end of the year no one was more surprised than I when I learned that I had been promoted to the fifth grade.

When we first started at Mentor School, we did not eat in the lunchroom. The one dollar a week per child that it cost was far too expensive for our family budget. This did not bother me because the school food was not good anyway. Mom's cooking was so much better. Mom packed our lunch, usually egg or potato pancake sandwiches, that we carried to school in brown paper bags. After the first year the government started a program that provided lunch to needy students. Under this program it only cost one dollar a week to feed all the family's children who attended school. With five of us in school it was a very good deal for our family, and that year we started eating with the other kids in the school lunch room.

We usually rode the school bus, but occasionally, on nice mornings, we would walk, which was not a big deal because we had to walk halfway to school just to catch the bus anyway. The bus stopped near the southeast corner of the Hultiquist farm on Topton Road, across from the Rowlands' house. When it rained we would wait in the Rowlands' living room until the bus came. Despite the fact that there were a lot of us—five Lamberts, three Robinsons, three Rowlands, and Mary Ellen Hicks—Mrs. Rowland was always good-natured and pleasant. She was an angel for putting up with us. I am sorry to say that, as far as I know, neither we children nor my parents ever bothered to thank her for taking care of us.

We were ashamed that we were Indians, so we did not let other kids know that we were enrolled in the Eastern Band of Cherokees. I even lied to hide my Indian background. One day Miss Johnnie had each student stand up and tell the class where they had been born. Worried that the students would laugh when I said Cherokee, I sat there dreading my turn. When my turn came, I cowardly avoided the problem by stating that I had been born in Bryson City. Then I just sat there holding my breath in fear that my sister Betty would say something. She was in the same room as I was, on the third-grade side. Thankfully, I don't think Betty was even paying attention to the fourth-grade side of the room. She said nothing. I sat down and hoped that Miss Johnnie would let it go at that. She did, and I let out a sigh of relief.

The kids at Mentor School still found out that we were Indian, and they teased us quite a bit. Robert Rowland was always reminding me that while he was 100 percent American, I was only part American since I was also part Indian. It didn't occur to me that this actually made me more American than he was.

My fifth-grade teacher was very good, but I did not like her. She was firm and did not smile much. Unlike in Miss Johnnie's class, if I wanted good grades I had to earn them, and some of the courses were very difficult indeed.

On my first report card of fifth grade I got a U for what she judged to be my unsatisfactory performance in forestry. In that class we learned about the plants and trees of Tennessee. Like a fool I thought that because I lived on a farm I already knew all there was to know about this topic. Instead I learned that I did not know much at all. I might have known many of the common names of the trees and plants, but I did not know their scientific names. When I started that class, I did not even know that they had scientific names, and boy, did those long, strange names throw me for a loop.

Mom really went off the handle when she saw that U on my report card. I tried to explain to her how difficult forestry turned out to be, but it was no use. Poor grades made Mom madder than anything I could think of. So after sulking for a while, I decided that that U would be my last. I studied that forestry book very hard and never received another U. I settled down, worked hard, and by the second half of the fifth grade I was well on my way. I had finally caught up with the other students.

In the sixth grade there were three grades in my schoolroom, sixth through eighth, instead of the two grades that most classrooms had. I think that a lot of kids had enrolled in the first grade, and there wasn't enough space for the second grade to share the same room with the first grade. Unlike the fifth grade, the sixth grade, I found, was very easy. My confidence was bolstered when I emerged as one of the better students in the class. I started to become involved in extracurricular activities. I joined the 4H club and excelled in my main project of growing strawberries.

In the sixth grade I also began to notice girls. I don't know why I didn't notice them earlier; maybe I was too worried about doing well in school, or it might have been that there were no pretty girls in my classes. In the sixth grade, however, I began to notice Jean Duff, a very pretty eighth-grader who lived on the edge of Mentor in a big white two-story house on a very prosperous farm. But there was no way I would have let her or anyone else know how I felt.

One day during lunch recess I was told to report to the teacher. I feared that I had done something wrong, but for the life of me I could not think of anything that I had done that warranted the teacher to summon me. Fearing the worst, I walked into the classroom. When I entered, my heart flipped. I saw my teacher with Jean Duff, who gave me the sweetest smile I had ever seen. I walked over to them, and our teacher came right to the point. He said that the 4H club was conducting a countywide contest. A team from each school would make a presentation about the importance of first aid, and the three teams that gave the best presentations would win a trip to the state 4H club convention in Nashville. He said that Jean wanted to represent Mentor School and that she wanted me to be her partner. Man alive, was I surprised. A three-day trip to Nashville with Jean Duff would be heaven. I began to fantasize about the trip and decided that a trip like that could lead to real romance. I must have been grinning from ear to ear when I said, "Yes, I would be glad to be Jean's partner."

The competition organizers had arranged for each presentation to include a twenty-minute discussion between the two team members about first aid. This would take place in front of an audience on a Saturday morning at the courthouse in Maryville. Our props were the contents of a first aid kit.

Our first practice sessions went fairly well. Jean was flawless. I, however, had some trouble. During the presentation I had to say, "Use merthiolate rather than mercurochrome." For some reason I had trouble saying "merthiolate." I practiced and practiced until I thought I had the pronunciation down pat.

The day of the competition arrived. I dressed in a clean pair of pants and a clean white short-sleeve shirt. Then the whole Lambert family headed off to the Maryville courthouse for the competition. Jean and I were up against six other teams.

I thought our presentation went very well, close to perfect. As usual Jean was flawless. But I did make one very small mistake. At the last minute I decided that I would be better off avoiding the word "merthiolate" altogether rather than risk mispronouncing it. Instead of following the proscribed text I said, "Use *this* for treatment of minor wounds rather than mercurochrome." When she heard me say *this*, Jean gave me a hard long look. When the judging was over, Jean and I came in fourth, just a few points short of third place. I am sure that that one little four-letter word cost us the few points that we needed to win that trip to Nashville. We each received a twenty-five-dollar war bond instead. Jean never spoke to me again.

My seventh-grade teacher, Mr. Coe, was an older, bald-headed man. There was nothing milk toast about this man, and he treated us firmly, much as a mean father would treat his children. He kept a big two-foot-long paddle on his desk in full view of everyone. I saw him use it several times right in front of the class as an example of what would happen to us if we misbehaved. Each morning when he rang the bell, we went directly to our seats in a very orderly fashion and sat quietly while he opened his Bible and read the thirteenth chapter of First Corinthians, verse 11: "When I was a child, I spoke as a child, I understood as a child, I thought as a child: but when I became a man, I put away childish things."

This was Mr. Coe's philosophy. Each morning he reminded us that we were no longer children and that he expected us to put away our childish ways and act like adults. We did our best to please him because we knew that if we did not please him, the paddle was waiting. After Mr. Coe read the Bible, he led us in singing the Tennessee state song and another song, usually "Onward Christian Soldiers," "Old Black Joe," or "The Little Brown Church in the Dale." Although he was strict, Mr. Coe was also a good teacher, and I really got my studies in high gear and made straight Es. This time I felt like I had earned them.

I went home from my first day in the eighth grade in a good mood. Our teacher, Mrs. Brown, a woman in her thirties, had entered the classroom with a wide smile and told us that this was going to be a fun school year. Unlike Mr. Coe she did not treat us like children. The first thing she did was to give us a talk about how we were to behave in the classroom. She made it clear that she was going to treat us as if we were adults. She promised us that we would learn a lot in the coming year. She also appeared to be rich in comparison with Mr. Coe because she drove a nice green 1941 Chevrolet to school. Mr. Coe drove a 1930 Model A Ford.

This class was made even better by the arrival of a slender, good-looking girl named Janice Clemons. Our room had two rows of eighth-grade desks, five in each row, and Janice chose one of the two front desks, the one closest to Mrs. Brown's desk. I was no dummy, so I chose a desk about two desks back in the other row. That seat gave me the best view of Janice.

With Mrs. Brown at the helm, and Janice well in view, we wasted no time and moved right into our studies. My initial opinion of our new teacher proved to be correct. She was a great teacher, and she was well aware that most of the students, with the exception of Janice, were a gaggle of farmers' children who had given little thought to the future. Her first objective was to make us think about what we were going to do after we finished high school. One day, soon after the first day of classes, she opened class by asking each of us what we expected to do. Most of the girls said they wanted to get married. The boys said that they were going to work on a farm. I decided that I would give her a big-shot intelligent answer and said that I wanted to be a truck driver. She looked at me sadly and said, "What a shame. What a waste of your talents. You should start thinking about college, and my task is to make you plan for college." Of course Janice gave her the right answer and said that she planned to go to college.

Mrs. Brown's remarks stayed with me, and I started thinking that someday maybe, just maybe, I could go to college. I thought how nice it would be to go to the University of Tennessee. However, I soon put those thoughts of college out of my mind and just started enjoying my last year at Mentor School.

My best friend, Robert Rowland, was a grade behind me. Janice, quite confident of herself, came right out and chose Robert to be her boyfriend. I don't think he even had a say in the matter. Still, it was clear that he was pleased as punch to have been chosen. One might think that I would have been upset that she had settled on Robert, but I wasn't. Robert and I were always hanging out together. This meant that when Janice was hanging around with Robert, she was also hanging around with me.

Each fall the school sponsored a two-month fund-raising event. In late September each room elected a King and a Queen who were responsible for collecting the money. The team that collected the most money would be crowned King and Queen of the school at a festival held in November. We elected Robert our King and Janice our Queen. Janice's mother took a real interest in Janice's activities, and it was clear that she intended to make sure that Janice and Robert would earn the title of King and Queen of the school. Janice's father was a foreman at ALCOA and made good money compared to the rest of the students' fathers. Everyone knew that her father was prepared to write a check for twenty-five or thirty dollars on festival night to make sure that Janice won.

Janice and Robert's romance seemed to be made in heaven. Here they were selected by the class to be King and Queen, and for the first six weeks they never argued. They were always lovey-dovey. Then, ten short days before the festival, their romance went sour, and Robert announced that he refused to be Janice's King. Boy, did I think Robert was stupid. And poor Janice, there she was: she had no King to escort her to the festival.

Early one morning before class, while I was warming myself by the classroom coal stove, I felt a gentle tap on my shoulder. I turned around to find myself looking into Janice's beautiful eyes. She gave me a big smile and said, "Hello, Leonard." I was tongue-tied. I stood there with a stupid smile on my face and mumbled something. Thank goodness, the bell rang. I walked on air to my desk and sat there feeling a warm glow in the cold schoolroom. I knew that Janice wanted me to be her new boyfriend, and I was thrilled to become that special person in Janice's life. That is, if I could get over being so bashful. Then I began to wonder how Robert would take it. I glanced over at Robert, who was sitting there fuming mad. Then I looked up the row to Janice. I decided that I did not care what Robert thought. He could beat me up over this for all I cared. After all, James Derrick had already done that to me, and it did not hurt that much. I passed that beautiful morning sitting at my desk dreaming of my impending romance.

By lunch my warm romantic feelings had passed, and I was playing softball when Mrs. Brown summoned me to the classroom. Once again I found myself wondering what I could have done wrong. When I got there, Mrs. Brown, Janice, and Janice's mother were deep in discussion. Mrs. Brown explained that Robert refused to be King because he was mad at Janice. She said that they had decided that I should take Robert's place. I told Mrs. Brown that I would be honored to be Janice's King. I figured that if Janice and I won King and Queen of the school, Janice would be my girl for the rest of the year, maybe forever.

I felt very good about being King, but in the back of my mind I realized that I had a problem. I had to tell Mom. That evening at the dinner table I told Mom and Dad what had happened at school that day. I also causally mentioned that I would need a suit for festival night. Dad ignored me. He said he was not interested in this school junk. Mom, however, just sat there getting madder and madder as she thought about "this great event that was about to take place in my social life," as I called it. Mom was no dummy. She asked me just how it came about that I was going to be King on such short notice. When I told her what had happened, she got as mad as an old sitting hen and lit into me. After ranting about how stupid I was for playing second fiddle, she came down to the facts. First, she said that we did not have five dollars to waste on a suit. I told her that I had the money, but that wasn't good enough for her. She said that

I was not going to waste her money or my money on a suit. Next, she said that if they wanted me to be King, I should have been the first pick, and not selected to fill in because Robert was in a tizzy. I thought about it, and I had to agree that Mom had a point.

I knew I was in a jam. I knew there was no way I was going to get a suit, and without a suit I could not go to the festival. Worse, if I did not go to the festival as Janice's King, our romance was over. Well, I decided to do what any other coward would have done.

Festival night was to be held the next Friday, about a week away. I decided to get sick Wednesday night and not go to school on Thursday or Friday. That Thursday, according to plan, I sent word to Mrs. Brown that I was sick and would not be able attend school on Thursday or Friday. I added that I would not be well enough on Friday evening to go to the festival. When they heard this, Mrs. Brown and Janice tried to get Robert to change his mind. But old Robert remained headstrong and stupid. He refused to even consider changing his mind. Desperate, they talked Charles Hunt into being King, and he agreed immediately. I guess he already had a suit, and maybe Charles wanted Janice as a girlfriend as much as I wanted her. Charles did get to be King, but he did not get Janice. When I returned to school after the festival, I found that my romance with Janice was already over. She completely ignored me, and it wasn't long before Janice and Robert had made amends. They spent the rest of the year on and off together, and I spent the rest of the year following them around.

In September of 1947 Janice went to Alcoa High School, and I went to Friendsville High School. The following year our family moved to Mars Hill, and I lost track of Janice. Robert told me later that Janice entered Friendsville High School during her sophomore year and chose Jack McNeilly as her boyfriend and that they were pretty serious. I have to admit that she chose well. Jack was a real nice good-looking guy and a very good student. His father owned a successful farm near Friendsville. That first year at Friendsville Jack and I were pretty good friends, and if I had gone to Friendsville as a sophomore he, Janice, and I could have hung around together, just as Robert, Janice, and I had done a couple of years before.

The school year at Mentor rolled along, and before we knew it, the end of the school year was at hand, and it was time to prepare for the eighth-grade graduation ceremony. Mrs. Brown told me that I was class valedictorian and Janice class salutatorian. She said that each of us would have to make a speech at the graduation ceremony. I panicked, and I asked Mrs. Brown where I could find a speech. Mrs. Brown said she wanted me to talk about atomic energy. I panicked again. I knew nothing about atomic energy except that it was used in bombs.

As it turned out, I did not have to worry about that speech anyway. Shortly after she learned that her daughter was salutatorian, Janice's mother came to school and spoke with Mrs. Brown. Then Mrs. Brown told me that she had made a mistake and that Janice was valedictorian and I was salutatorian. I said that it was all right with me. But it wasn't all right with Mom. When I told her about the mistake, she got even madder than when I told her that I had been invited to stand in for Robert as King. Eventually Mom settled down and accepted the idea that being salutatorian was still an honor.

The graduation was a big deal. It was held at night in the Mentor Methodist Church. Mom and Dad shelled out $7.50 to buy me a suit to wear. In addition I did make a speech. It was a canned speech that Mrs. Brown gave me called "All's Well That Ends Well." I finished speaking and sat down. After the applause had settled, I decided I had done a good job. When I thought about what I had said, I decided that it was true. In life all's well that ends well.

In late August I boarded the bus and went to enroll at Friendsville High School. The bus came down Topton Road, went to Mentor, to Louisville, and then on to Friendsville. It took about three hours to go to and from school, making the day long indeed. I would leave home at seven in the morning and get back at five in the evening, just in time to do some chores. On some days I had time to milk the cows before I left for school in the morning.

On the first day, as we went through Mentor on our way to Friendsville, I looked for Janice as we passed her house. I hoped that she had changed her mind about going to Alcoa High School. I did not see her. After I enrolled, I got right to work and did very well. My most interesting courses were science and math. This was an uneventful school year that ended in May, just as Dad was starting to make plans to move the family to Mars Hill.

With the war winding down, the price of goods started to rise rapidly. During the war most people made good money and saved a lot of it because there was little to buy. At the end of the war in 1945 jobs on production lines were paying about a dollar an hour, $160 a month. But our family did not benefit from this. Dad was still making the same $75 monthly salary that he had started with in January 1943. He never shared in any farm profits because there were none. It was getting harder for our family to make ends meet. To make matters worse, we children were getting older and more expensive for Mom and Dad.

Several years earlier Dad had tried to improve our situation by looking into buying our own farm in Tennessee. He started looking at farms for sale and went so far as to apply for and get preliminary approval for a government farm loan. Dad was interested in a hundred-acre farm toward Friendsville, out in the middle of nowhere. The farm had an old rundown house and a barn, but it had neither livestock nor equipment. The land was flat, looked rundown, and did not appear fertile. The seller wanted five thousand dollars, a fortune for us and a price that Dad decided he could not afford. I think his decision to stay with Victor was a good one, even if we were just sinking deeper and deeper into poverty.

Mom did what she could to help. She cut our expenses by continuing to make clothes from feed sacks. She also made Indian crafts, mainly beadwork and Indian dolls, and every three months she took the bus to Gatlinburg to sell them. On each trip she earned about twenty-five dollars. Not much, but it did help us make ends meet.

Eventually, Dad agreed to let Mom take a job in a greasy spoon cafe on Highway 129, just north of the airport. Dad took Mom to work each day in time for the afternoon shift, and he picked her up when she got off at ten in the evening. It was a hard day for both of them as they both got up at five in the morning. Mom did all her household chores before going to work in the afternoon. Despite the long days Mom did like going to work as it allowed her to get away from the farm for a while each day.

Dad wasn't as happy, and he quickly learned that what goes around comes around. When we lived in the cove, Dad happily went off to work each day with his fire rake over his shoulder, and Mom had to stay home looking after the kids. While he was away, Mom would sit there imagining that Dad was seducing all sorts of women as he wandered around the countryside looking for forest fires. This is exactly what Dad had to go through every day that Mom went off to work. Dad had to stay on the farm in the afternoons working, taking care of children, and building visions of all the strange men who were cozying up to Mom at the cafe. Each evening he would finish the chores, feed us the supper that Mom had prepared, wash the dishes, and then head off to the cafe at about seven.

He would sit in the cafe until Mom got off at ten, watching her as she served customers. This was the type of cafe where chatting with the waitress came with the greasy food. As Dad sat in the cafe, he would watch Mom talk and flirt with customers, and he would get madder and madder. I doubt he ever said anything to Mom about this while she was working, but he sure did say a lot on the way home. That they were both very tired only made matters worse.

By the time they came through our door at ten-thirty, they would be well into a heated argument. All us kids would wake up and urge them to make peace, usually to no avail. After a while, very late at night, they would get too tired to fight, and we would all go to sleep.

This fighting affected all us children. Not only did we wet our beds, but we starting having nightmares again—the same kind of nightmares as we had had in the cove. I remember one three-month stretch during which Don had horrible nightmare every night. Don would be in a trance, and he would start talking crazy. His whole body would go rigid, and he would have a wild look in his eyes, which were wide open. I suppose I reacted the same way when I had my nightmares. This wildness would last about fifteen minutes or so, and then Don would come out of it, drained and frightened. He could not remember any of the nightmares, except that something very scary and indescribable had happened. After those nightmares it took quite some time before we were able to return to bed. Even fifty years later Don continues to have these nightmare trances, and he does not even have to be sleeping for them to strike. They can strike at any time, and even today when he comes out of these spells, he remembers hearing Dad saying that he was going to leave the family.

Mom's working might have fueled those fights, but it did not make us rich. We were still getting poorer and poorer. By 1948 our standard of living had sunk to the bare minimum. From 1943 to 1948 inflation was steady at about 7 percent a year. By then the purchasing power of Dad's seventy-five-dollar monthly paycheck had sunk by a third, to fifty-three dollars.

In the spring of 1948 Boyd Hampton, Mom's brother-in-law, wrote to Dad and told him that Mars Hill College needed a painter. Boyd had told the Mars Hill maintenance superintendent, Bryson Tilson, that Dad would be a good man for the job. Dad immediately went to Mars Hill and got this job that would pay him about two hundred dollars per month.

Dad came back to the farm and gave Victor notice that we were moving to Mars Hill, a small town just to the northwest of Asheville, at the end of June. Victor did not like the idea of us leaving and immediately offered Dad $125 a month to stay on the farm. Dad thought it over, but in the end he decided to take the new job in Mars Hill.

I had just turned sixteen. I was old enough to understand how much better off we could have been if only the farm had lived up to its potential. I left the farm with disdain for Victor. For five years he used us as his servants. We were peons on his show farm. People were supposed to get richer as they moved along in life. But we just became poorer and poorer. That June, in 1948, we were much poorer than we had been in 1943, when we first moved to the farm. We followed his orders for five years for a measly seventy-five dollars a month, and we never even uttered one complaint.

Now, looking back, I feel that maybe we were to blame for our situation. It was not just that Victor did not help us; it was also that when we moved to the farm in 1943, we were not just very poor; we were also dumb and ignorant. Mom and Dad did not know how to take advantage of all the opportunities that the farm had to offer. I guess Victor just figured that he got what he paid for, and he assumed that we were happy because we never complained. The farm was exactly what he wanted it to be: a showplace. To be honest, the only reason we never complained is because we never knew what to complain about.

Over time my feelings toward Victor have softened, and today my feelings toward him are conflicting. On one hand I liked Victor because he did take good care of us by letting us have the run of the farm and never withholding Dad's seventy-five-dollar monthly salary. Victor was an honorable, honest man. I sometimes think that if Dad had accepted Victor's last offer and we had stayed on the farm, our economic situation might have improved greatly. Sometimes I even think that Victor might have helped my siblings and me attend college and that with his guidance we might have accomplished more in school. But really, would Victor have helped us in these ways? I doubt it. Still, Victor always came through when Dad asked him for a favor. He was kind, like when he took us to Cherokee when Grandma died and when he offered to let us live in one of his houses if Dad were drafted. And he did keep Dad out of the army.

One day, many years later, I had a conversation with Mom about our years on the farm. When I expressed ill feelings about Victor, Mom jumped on me. She said that Victor was one of the best people she had ever known because he kept Dad alive by keeping him out of the army. I had to admit that she was probably right. I just shut up and stopped talking about Victor.

In 1960, when my wife, Julia, and I were living in Calderwood, we went to see the Hultiquists at their home in Alcoa. Mrs. Hultiquist was as lively as could be, but Victor had grown old and feeble. He just sat there in the living room chair and didn't say much. Sometime after our visit someone drove the Hultiquists to Calderwood to see us. They showed us the house where they had lived in the 1920s and 1930s. Not long after this visit to Calderwood, they moved into the Methodist retirement home near Maryville. I never saw them again.

Mars Hill

In late June 1948 we loaded our few belongings onto a stake-bed truck, packed into our 1934 Chevrolet, and headed for Mars Hill. We were full of confidence and excited that we were moving to a real town. Another plus for us was that we would not be far from Cherokee. With tourism booming on the reservation, we looked forward to eventually moving back to Cherokee and taking advantage of the new opportunities that were there. Shortly after we arrived in Mars Hill, Dad borrowed fifteen hundred dollars and bought Grandma Lambert's old farm in Birdtown from Philip. Dad had plans to build a tourist gift shop on the road frontage.

When we drove into Mars Hill, I imagine us as having looked like the Joad family in John Steinbeck's novel *The Grapes of Wrath*. Well, we might not have been quite as down and out as that family, but we sure were close to it. The house that Dad's boss let us use until we could find another was located one short block west of Main Street, right in the center of Mars Hill. I often wonder what the people of Mars Hill thought when they saw us drive right into the center of town packed into our 1934 Chevy, trailed by a flatbed truck that carried all that we owned.

Then and today Mars Hill is a small college town whose two-block downtown is little more than an extension of the college. The town had a small cafe, post office, gas station, general store, donut shop, movie theater, dry cleaner, hardware store, florist, dentist, doctor, fire truck, two grocery stores, and a drug store that had a soda fountain operated by the high school principal's wife.

This town was sized just right for our dog Fido, and he knew it from the first day we arrived. When I worked in a grocery store in the middle of town, I would often look out the window and see him prancing up and down the sidewalk with a strut that suggested that he thought he owned the town. He spent a lot of time hanging out on a sunny sidewalk corner, daring any other dog to show its face. After we moved up to High School Ridge, poor Fido was injured when he was run over by a car. Dad had one of his workers take Fido up to the water reservoir. I never saw him again.

We were not alone in Mars Hill. Years earlier Helen, Mom's sister, had married Boyd Hampton, a non-Indian, with whom she had two children—Philip and Joyce. Boyd and Helen lived about halfway between Mars Hill and Marshall, on the old Hampton farm. Boyd's mentally retarded brother, Milt, and a sister lived in the old farmhouse and tilled the farm. Boyd, who got Dad his job, had for a long time worked as a painter at Mars Hill College. Helen really moved up in life when she married Boyd. She was able to leave the reservation and live with her husband, who had a very good job; at least it was a good job when compared to the jobs held by my other relatives.

I can't say that Mom was crazy about living near Helen. She did not like her at all. The ill feelings were probably mutual, because Helen likely knew that Mom had carried on with Boyd when she was younger. If Mom and Helen had acted like mature adults, they would have gotten over all this stuff by the time we moved to Mars Hill. But I guess in all of us there is a little piece that just won't grow up.

Mom always said that Helen was snobbish and acted like she was above her upbringing. Helen used to take a bus to shop in Asheville. When she returned, she would come to our house waving her Ivey's shopping bags around and wait with us until her husband got off work. This made Mom furious. She claimed that Helen was just showing off by strutting around with those Ivey's bags. Mom claimed that Helen didn't really shop at Ivey's. She said that Helen would just fill those bags with junk she had picked up at a dime store.

For several years Mom even refused to speak to Helen. In 1963, when Helen was in the hospital dying, Mom decided to break her silence and went to visit her, but Phil and Joyce, Helen's children, told Mom that Helen was too sick to see her. But I don't believe it. I think Helen just did not want to see Mom.

Helen's son, Philip, worked his way through Berea College, earned a degree in geology, and became a successful engineer and company manager. In 1989 the Michigan professional engineering organization even recognized his accomplishments by naming him Engineer of the Year. I was working in Detroit at that time, and I had a chance to spend some time with Philip. I was impressed by how smart he was. Later I told Mom that I thought Philip was the most accomplished and intelligent of my generation. Boy, did she hit the ceiling. Even though Helen had been dead for so many years, I could see that Mom still held a grudge against her.

Bryson Tilson, Dad's new boss, was superintendent of the Mars Hill College maintenance department, and he was kind enough let Dad rent a college-owned house until the end of August. It was an old, old house located one block from the center of town. It was on Marshall Highway, across the road from the Mars Hill Dry Cleaners. It had three bedrooms, a living room, kitchen, toilet, dining room, and front and back porches. This house was much more comfortable than our old house on the farm and the house that Dad had built in the cove. Unfortunately, we knew that we would have to find other housing by the end of August, as the college used the house for student housing during the school year.

In 1948 many veterans were attending college on the Servicemen's Readjustment Act of 1944, a bill popularly referred to as the GI Bill. This act provided unemployment and education allowances, along with loans for homes, farms, and businesses for returning war veterans. Because of the influx of veterans, Mars Hill College, like most colleges and universities, was bursting at the seams with students. The community could comfortably accommodate about eight hundred students. That year the college enrollment swelled to twelve hundred.

As you can imagine, rental housing was hard to find. The college did all it could to house students by converting some faculty houses into rooms for students. Students were tripled up in rooms designed for two, and there was little housing in Mars Hill left for large families like ours.

As soon as we settled into our house, Dad started looking for a permanent place for us to live, a difficult task indeed. In spite of the housing situation Dad did find a small two-bedroom house about a half mile from town. He did not take the house the day he found it because it was still early in August, and he wanted to see if he could find a bigger and cheaper place before the end of the month.

My cousin Phil Hampton was working for the maintenance department when we arrived in Mars Hill, and Bryson Tilson immediately hired me to help Phil wash windows and wax floors during the summer. Each day after work I helped with household chores, and then I would wander around the campus, where I would meet up with the college's night watchman, with whom I spent hours sitting on the curb talking.

At that time the night watchman was living in a three-room shack about one mile from town, on the road toward Asheville. It was a rundown house hardly fit for anyone. It had a front room, a bedroom, and a large kitchen. Its only heat came out of a fireplace in the front room. A privy was located about one hundred feet behind the house. The only redeeming feature of the house was that water was piped into the kitchen.

One night after work I was sitting on the curb talking with the night watchman, and I stupidly told him about the house Dad had found. Well, that no-good night watchman rented the house right out from under us the very next day. Not knowing that he had rented our house, I looked for the night watchman the next several nights and could not find him, and I wondered what had happened to him. Then I found out what he had done, and I knew that he was hiding from me. Dad wouldn't find out what had happened until about a week later, when he went to sign the lease. Talk about mad. That time I could hardly blame Mom and Dad for yelling at me.

Well, now we were in a real bind, as we could not find another house to rent. Dad ended up renting the rundown shack where the night watchman had been living. It was a tight fit, but we managed to live there for about six months. The old rundown shack was located right next door to the home of Dr. Otis Duck and his wife. Years later Mom and Dad would be buried in the Mars Hill cemetery, right next to Dr. Otis Duck.

The college owned a lot of land in and around Mars Hill, including farmland. Bryson Tilson let us use the college pasture and barn for our cows and chickens. Dad built a pigpen behind the barn for our pig. We chose a couple of nice fields for our gardens.

Once again we were set to make a lot of money, and this time we did pretty well. I started work that summer, and once school started, Bryson let me continue working each day after school and on Saturdays. The college paid me fifty cents an hour. All the older members of the family also went to work; Betty worked for the telephone company, and Mom went to work in the school cafeteria.

To earn some extra cash, Dad and I took over the task of operating the film projector for the students. On Tuesdays, Thursdays, and Saturdays, when no drama or music programs were scheduled, the college showed movies in the auditorium. When we arrived in Mars Hill, Orville Howell operated the projector. He worked as the electrical repairman for the college and owned a radio repair business that he operated at night and on weekends. This work kept him busy enough, so he was eager to pass responsibility for operating the projector to someone else. When Dad was offered the job, he jumped at the opportunity. Orville trained him in the projector operation, and then Dad trained me. Then we took over showing movies.

I think that I enjoyed working in the maintenance department even more than showing the movies. The work was much easier and more enjoyable than farmwork. Best of all, I was able to work with someone my age. This was the first time that I had someone other than Dad to talk with while I was working. Now think about that. I was sixteen years old and had never had anyone to really talk with while

I was working. You cannot imagine how good it made me feel to work with Phil.

Phil and I worked well together. Phil was smart, and I learned a lot from him. For instance, one day we were talking about outer space. He said that the sun was ninety-three million miles from earth and that the moon was about a quarter million miles from earth. I said that I was not sure about that because I had heard many preachers say that most of this so-called science was a lot of nonsense and the work of the devil because science conflicted with the Bible. I added that the preachers claimed that the moon was just as far away from earth as the stars. They said that if you looked closely you could see the stars streaking across the face of the moon. After he heard this, Phil looked at me like I was a fool. He said, "Leonard, what people see streaking across the face of the moon are not stars but meteorites, and the moon is really only about a quarter million miles from the earth, and the nearest star is about four million light years away." As I said, I learned a lot from Phil.

As things turned out, Dad was not a good painter. When the grounds foreman quit, Bryson Tilson promoted Dad to foreman. This was right down Dad's alley. Taking care of the grounds was just like working on a farm.

Dad got a small raise, and we moved into the former foreman's house, which was right across the road from the Science Building, where Bryson's office and the maintenance shop were located. Although the house was small, it had four regular-size rooms and a small fifth room; the house was a big improvement over the shack in which we had been living. The house had city water in the kitchen, but no bathroom. A privy was behind the house, on the lower edge of one of our gardens. For me the best thing was that the house was downtown.

We lived in that house for about a year. Then, in late 1949, Bryson allowed Dad to rent one of the larger houses on campus that was located up the street from the Science Building. Our neighbor was Harvey "Pop" Lance, who taught pre-engineering and math. The house had a living room, three bedrooms, a kitchen, a dining room, a half bath, and a full bath. We even had a driveway for our car. By then Dad had saved enough money to trade our 1934 Chevy for a 1947 Chevy Fleetline. We were really coming up in the world. Later Dad bought our first TV set. It received one channel, WBTV from Charlotte.

Dad really liked his new job and took to it as a fish takes to water. He supervised a crew of about fifteen workmen who did all the grounds maintenance. He also supplied workers whenever any of the departments needed additional labor. Two or three black workers, who lived in a small black village about a mile from Mars Hill, were in Dad's crew. A few women from there worked in the college cafeteria. In the 1950s few blacks lived west or north of Asheville, and I knew of no blacks living west of Soco Gap in Cherokee.

My father grew up in an area where there were no blacks, and along with most Indians he did not like them, or at least he believed that they had their place and that they should stay there. I doubt that Dad was bothered that a few blacks worked in his crew; after all he was their boss. However, I guess the blacks sensed that Dad still harbored racist attitudes. One black worker in Dad's crew was a young six-foot-six black man named Pink. He was easygoing and a steady worker. He cut the grass on a big riding mower.

One day all the blacks were working in the same area of campus when Dad came by to check on their progress. While there he gave Pink an order with an air that made Pink fume with anger. He said that he did not like Dad's tone of voice and that he refused to take this kind of order from a white man. Dad fired Pink on the spot. Outraged, all the blacks quit working and marched to Bryson's office. Poor Dad just stood there wondering how he had gotten himself into such a mess. Once he had gathered his thoughts, Dad gathered the tools, and then he climbed onto Pink's mower and drove it back to the maintenance office.

Bryson and the black workmen were waiting for Dad by the time he arrived. Bryson took Dad into his office and told him that he did not have the authority to hire and fire workers. Bryson added that only he had that authority. Bryson also told Dad that if he wanted to keep his job, he had to undo the firing. What a predicament for Dad. He had to apologize to a black man. I am proud to say that Dad did as he was told and found a way to make peace with the blacks who worked for him.

I am sure that deep inside Dad was boiling mad, but he kept his cool, and he never again gave the blacks any trouble. In return the blacks never gave Dad any trouble either. But that would not be the last time that Dad got into trouble at work.

During Halloween male college students let off steam by wandering around campus and making a nuisance of themselves. Usually their pranks were minor, but the college administration still frowned on this activity. One year Dean Lee and the administration decided that there would not be a Halloween celebration. Bryson Tilson enlisted all his maintenance men to help the night watchman maintain order. Of course Dad volunteered to help. The students, aware of the plan, began to look forward to the night's activities. Almost all the male students showed up to confront the maintenance workers.

I knew nothing about what happened on campus that Halloween night until I arrived at high school the following morning. One of my friends said that it was too bad about what had happened at the college the night before. I asked him what had happened, and he was very surprised that I did not know. Later that afternoon I would learn the details as to what had transpired the night before.

Around midnight a large group of male students gathered in front of the administration building and started raising all kinds of hell. A few members of the Tilson Brigade, including my father, ordered the group to break up and return to the dorms. The students taunted the brigade and then took off running up the street toward the center of town. The brigade took off in pursuit. Dad was right in the middle of the fracas and took off after one of the larger students. Dad caught up with him and planted his three-cell stainless-steel flashlight right in the back of the student's head. The student crumpled into a motionless heap. I guess Dad thought the student was dead. One of the night watchmen checked the student and found that Dad had only knocked him out.

In a matter of minutes Bryson Wilson, Dean Lee, and President Blackwell were on the scene. As the downed student came to, the night watchmen explained what had happened. After hearing the story, Dean Lee told the students to return to their rooms and that he would investigate the matter the next day. The dean also warned the students that he might decide to expel the students who were involved. The students could see that Dean Lee meant business and that it would be wise not to give him any backtalk, lest they be expelled on the spot. The unruly scene calmed down, and the night watchman took the injured student to the infirmary. Lucky for Dad, the nurse found that all the student had was a big bump on the back of his head. Other than that he was fine. I guess the student also had one hell of a headache.

The next day Dad, Dean Lee, and Bryson discussed the incident and decided that Dad should apologize to the student, which my dad did. Dad was happy that the administration let the matter drop and hoped that all involved would soon forget the incident. I guess the administration soon forgot the incident. The students, however, did not.

One night, two weeks after Halloween, the students got their revenge. They knew that Dad kept his cow in the college barn. Around midnight a couple of students went to the barn and led Dad's cow to the administration building. They led her up a long flight of stairs to the second floor, under the bell tower, where they tied the school-bell rope around her neck. Then they hightailed it back to their rooms and waited.

The school bell was a big bell that anyone on campus could hear. At three in the morning she began to toll. The night watchman went to the administration building and found the cow. He immediately came to tell Dad, and then he and Dad hurried back to rescue the cow. I am sure Dad cursed the students with each step. He was also probably wishing that he had laid his flashlight up against a few more heads.

Rescuing the cow was difficult indeed. It was a lot easier for the students to get the cow up the stairs than it was for Dad to get her back down. When Dad led the cow down the stairs, she got a bit excited and made quite a mess. After a few hours Dad led the cow out of the building and back to the barn. Then he went back to the administration building and cleaned up the mess. I am sure that the students enjoyed talking about Dad and his cow the next day. That year everyone on campus got to know my dad.

I loved the old house that we first lived in at Mars Hill. It was a lot bigger than our house in Tennessee, and it was also in the center of town, so close that our back porch was only about one hundred feet from the Mars Hill Baptist Church. In my spare time I started attending that church. The preacher, Reverend Soderman, was a good preacher, and he did a great job ministering to the students. He knew what it was that made students click. The church was always full of students. In addition to being a good speaker Reverend Soderman was also a good musician. At every service he would sit in front of the pulpit and perform a hymn on a carpenter's saw. He would bend the saw and stroke it with his bow. The twangy sound of his music was haunting.

Truth be told, many students came to church for reasons other than to hear Reverend Soderman's sermons. Some idealistic students came because they were interested in ministering to the rural poor in the immediate area. But many more came because it was the only place where they could date girls. The college did not even allow students to take their dates to see a movie in the theater that was just across the street from the college. In fact a male student could not walk into town with a girl.

The preacher knew that my family lived near the church, and he must have been puzzled that only I and not the rest of the family attended church. I know that Mom would have never considered stepping into such a high-falutin' church. It didn't matter to me. As far as I was concerned, one church is just like another. Anyway, one day the Reverend Soderman decided to come to our house and invite Mom and Dad to the service. Early one Sunday morning I went out on the back porch, and I saw him opening the gate to our backyard. Mom, who was standing in the kitchen, saw him at about the same time, and she bolted out of the kitchen, stormed past me, and opened the back-porch screen door. She angrily stared the preacher down and asked him what he thought he was doing in her backyard. He introduced himself and invited the whole family to church that morning. She said something real nasty to him and then told the preacher that she would never step foot into his church and ordered him to get out of her yard and to never even think of coming to her house again.

I cringed as I saw the disappointed and shocked expression on Reverend Soderman's face. He did not come to the house again, and neither Mom nor Dad ever went to his church or any other church for that matter. My mom had a way of taking charge, as she did when she chased off Preacher Soderman. She could be a hard woman.

Nor did Mom save all her wrath for Preacher Soderman. She was also hard on Dad, and needless to say, they continued to fight. As I was away at college for some of the time we lived in Mars Hill, I had some relief from our caustic home. My sister Helen has assured me that their fights in Mars Hill were as bad, if not worse, than they had ever been. Apparently Mom and Dad had one real blowout that climaxed with Dad's scripted threat to leave. There he stood with his hand on the door knob, when Mom said something that pushed Dad to make good on his words. He grabbed his hat, walked through the door, and drove off in his pickup truck.

Mom didn't know what to do. This wasn't in the script that they had been rehearsing for so many years. Helen said that Mom just sat there in shock in the living room for a while. Then she said that they would have to go find Dad. They went out, got in the car, and headed for Asheville.

When they got to Weaverville, they saw Dad in his pickup heading back toward Mars Hill. They turned around and followed him home.

In the tenth grade I thought that I wanted to be a football star. Football practice, however, proved a lot harder, more time consuming, and much less enjoyable than I expected it would be. After two weeks I quit. I thought that working would be a better use of my time, so I started working a couple of hours after school each day and five hours on Saturday. Watching my bank account steadily grow was a lot more satisfying than being a football star.

Whenever I wasn't working, I was usually with Bill Edwards, my best friend. Bill, the son of one of my teachers, lived in town, and we could be at each other's house in a matter of minutes. We both loved country music, and we followed the careers of all the country music stars. Bill was also a pretty good musician in his own right. He could play the guitar, piano, fiddle, and just about any other instrument he picked up. I tried to learn the guitar, but I soon realized that I had no musical talent whatsoever. We remained close until we both went off to North Carolina State College, where we started to drift apart.

I was a good student in high school and graduated with a high grade point average. Still, this was not Mentor School, and I did not finish at the top of the class. Of our class of fifty-four students there were five students who ranked higher than I did. In addition to being a good student, and despite quitting the football team, I was also popular among my fellow students. In the eleventh grade I was elected class president. I even managed to have a few girlfriends.

I met my first girlfriend shortly after I arrived in Mars Hill. I was working a lot, so I had money, but I still didn't have many friends. I spent much of my spare time watching movies alone at the local theater. I didn't go just to see the movies, but also to see the pretty, slender red-headed girl who worked behind the refreshment counter. When I went I made a point of going up to the counter to talk to her. But all I could muster up to say were the few words I needed to order a bag of popcorn. Luckily, I got a second chance to speak with her. When I enrolled in the tenth grade, I learned that we were in the same grade.

I learned that her name was Patricia Louise George. She lived in town near the cemetery. I also learned that she had a boyfriend, Hal Buckner. To make matters worse, Hal was older, in the eleventh grade, owned a new Chevrolet, and was a star football player. Whenever I walked out of the school building and saw his beautiful shiny four-door red Chevy, I burned with envy. Before long I was also burning with envy because he had Patty Lou.

Over the school year my attraction to Patty Lou only increased. I eventually mustered up the nerve to ask her to a movie, and she stunned me by saying yes. Mars Hill is a small town where everyone knows everyone's business, and I knew that word of our date would get back to Hal and that they would break up. Well, this is what happened, and Patty and I dated for about a month. Then we broke up, and she went back to Hal. Then a while later she left Hal and came back to me. This was how my relationship with Patty and Hal continued though three years of high school and four years of college.

She would choose Hal, then she would choose me, then she would choose Hal, then she would choose me. When Hal or I was waiting in the wings, we were always ready to step in when Patty was ready to change partners. All she had to do was crook her little finger at either of us, and we would come running back to her. Once after a football game during our senior year I had a minor car accident while Patty and I were out on a date. She was not impressed by my driving skills, quit dating me for a while, and went back to Hal. A little later she came to me and said that she wanted to go wreck another car.

I was not aware of it at the time, but during my third year at North Carolina State College, Patty and Hal broke up for the last time. Later I would learn that Hal had moved away from Mars Hill and married another girl. When I came home in late summer after my junior year, Patty Lou crooked her little finger at me. I came running for her harder than ever. That summer Patty Lou was much more serious about our relationship than she had ever been. But for some reason it seemed to me that something was missing. It wasn't fun anymore.

When I visited home during the first semester of my senior year, I continued to date her. We also spent quite a bit of time together during the Christmas holidays. But our relationship still was not the same as it once had been. I think our problem was that we were all alone and all of our friends had disappeared. We did not have Hal to make our relationship interesting. Now that we were truly to-gether and alone, we learned that we had nothing in com-mon. I began to feel hemmed in, and I actually found myself wishing that Hal would come and rescue me, as he had al-ways done in the past. Patty was always trying to talk to me about our future, and I knew in my heart that we were not going to have one.

Being the coward that I am, I just could not bring myself to end our relationship in person. I returned to Raleigh in early January, and I sat down and wrote her a "Dear John" letter. I felt like a cad. She answered my letter and said that she knew that the letter was on the way. She felt that some-thing was wrong while we were together during the holi-days. Her letter made me feel better. I think our romance had become a burden to her as well.

During the spells that Patty Lou was with Hal, I dated sev-eral other girls. One was Shirley Reeves, a girl whose family had moved to Mars Hill from Brooklyn, New York, during the summer of 1949. As a New York girl Shirley certainly knew her way around and was very confident. She was also good-looking and very friendly. When she arrived she looked around and decided that she wanted me to be her boyfriend. I willingly obliged. She lived with a very large family, including her sixty-five-year-old father and her older brother and his family. I do not know why they moved from New York, but the Reeves family faced the same housing crunch as we did. They moved into a small rundown house at the head of a cove and the end of a dirt road that intersected with the gravel California Creek road.

During the eleventh grade I went to work at Harry Well's grocery store. Harry ran a tight ship and thought that everyone in Mars Hill should shop at his store. Shirley and her family would come to town on Saturday afternoon to shop for groceries, but they did not shop at Harry's store. Instead they shopped at another store across the street. Many a Saturday Harry would stand at his store window and watch this large family go into his competitor's store and come out loaded with groceries. He would become upset that he was missing out on this business, and he would try to get me to use my influence with Shirley to get her family to buy groceries from him. Sometimes Shirley would walk across the street to Harry's store and talk with me while her family was shopping. During these visits Harry would be all sugar and cream, but Shirley's family never bought anything at Harry's store.

During my senior year of high school Shirley and her family moved to Walnut, a town about sixteen miles from Mars Hill. Then, after I started at North Carolina State, she and her family moved back to Brooklyn. I continued to date her off and on through my third year in college, as she frequently returned to Asheville to visit her aunt. Just before the spring holidays, during my first year at State, she wrote from Brooklyn and begged me to come to New York during spring break. I really had a burning desire to go to New York, and I tried to think of some way to get the money for the trip. But I had no money to spare, and I was too scared to ask Mom for it. I knew what my mom would say, and I did not want to go through her browbeating. I turned down her offer, and I went home to dull old Mars Hill for the holidays.

Going Home

In 1951, on my last day of high school, Dad and I went to Cherokee to build a gift shop on Dad's property in Birdtown. Tourism in Cherokee was booming, and we thought we could make a lot of money selling Indian crafts. Well, we did not make a lot of money, but we did make some.

It took three weeks to build the shop, after which Dad returned to his job at Mars Hill. I stayed in Cherokee to trim the construction and open the shop. I made a big yellow sign that read "OCONALUFTEE TRADING POST" and mounted it in a tall maple tree. The shop was nothing fancy. The building was about thirty by sixteen feet, with a small living area partitioned off from the shop. After our renter moved out of Grandma Lambert's house, we removed the partition and used the whole building for the shop.

A few days after we opened, a big green Buick Roadmaster pulled up. Mr. Block, a craft salesman from Knoxville, climbed out of the car, came into the shop, looked around, and proclaimed that we needed more stock. I told him that anyone could see that, but that we didn't have enough money to keep the shelves full. He said that he could solve that problem and added that he was willing to stock the shop on credit. I accepted his offer. Within two days six hundred dollars' worth of Japanese-made Indian artifacts arrived. The first summer we did pretty well. We paid off our debt and put about six hundred dollars in the bank. We also had enough stock remaining to open the shop the following year.

Managing the shop was fun. I enjoyed being on the reservation again. My sisters, Betty and Helen, got jobs at the outdoor drama *Unto These Hills*. Betty worked in the ticket office during the day, and Helen worked at the Mountain-side Theater at night. Two of us worked in the shop at all times. During the second summer I took one hundred dollars of my hard-earned cash and bought a 1931 Model A Ford so that we would have transportation. Since I had no boss, I took time each day to swim in the Oconaluftee River, which ran down the valley right across the road from the shop. Other than that, I tended the shop, which we kept open from seven in the morning to eleven in the evening.

I still needed an "Indian chief" to stand in front of the shop to attract the tourists. I bought a fifteen-dollar Indian headdress and hired a young man, Locust, for the job. I paid him a dollar a day and let him keep his tips. He didn't make much in the way of tips because he was more interested in drinking than he was in working. Every now and then he would walk to our cellar and take a sip from the jar of moonshine that he kept there. He was nice enough to offer me a sip now and them. I politely declined as I was not yet a drinker. Locust "chiefed" for a while, but he eventually quit for another job. Then Tom, one of my classmates at Birdtown School, asked me if he could take over the job.

To be honest, Tom never really wanted to be a "chief." But he wanted the job so that he could sell his moonshine. Every couple of weeks Tom would take off for a few days, go to his still, and make a run of moonshine. Then he would chief in front of my shop. I can't tell you how many times I would see a car pull into our parking lot, and I would get excited, expecting a customer to come in and buy something. Then Tom would go over to the car and talk with the driver for a minute, and the car would pull out and go on down the road. I know that these tourists were just looking for liquor, and Tom was sending them down the road to a house where his moonshine was sold. I am sure that Tom made more money selling moonshine than I did selling crafts.

In the 1940s Tom married another one of my old schoolmates. They lived in a little cove at the head of Kate Lambert Branch. Although Tom had a job, his wife, who worked in a shop in downtown Cherokee, was the family's main breadwinner. They lived just above Tom's father-in-law and his large family.

Tom was a womanizer, and he told me many stories about his conquests. I thought that his most interesting story was how he would watch his father-in-law's house and wait until everyone had left except his wife's younger sister. Then he would go down to his father-in-law's house and play around with her.

I had many friends in Cherokee. Many of these people would come by in the evening and spend a lot of time just sitting around talking. One old Indian, Epps, would come by every afternoon at five-thirty. Epps worked as an Indian chief, and for a small fee he would let tourists use his bow and arrows. He had carved a handsome bow out of locust wood, and he knew I would not be able to resist buying it and a few arrows for fifteen dollars.

I put a couple of bales of hay against a bank in front of the house and placed a target on the front of the bales. As I had a lot of spare time, I practiced until I was a good shot and could hit the bull's-eye about half of the time. When Epps would stop by on his way home, we would bet a quarter on who was a better shot. Epps always won. I guess he had a lot of spare time too. Walter also came by the shop every day. Walter, a good friend of Tom, lived about half-way up Kate Lambert Branch. Each evening Walter would come down the road from his house and sit on the shop porch and talk.

June, who was several years younger than Walter, lived in the next house down the road from him. Walter, having a keen eye for a good-looking woman, liked June's wife a lot more than he should have. Walter said that he used to slip over to June's house at night, stay at the edge of the woods, several yards from the house, and make sounds like a hoot owl. When June's wife heard him, she would tell June that she had to go to the outhouse. Then she would come outside to meet Walter. I doubt that June was fooled. Walter told me that when the draft board called June into the service, June asked Walter to take care of his wife while he was away. Walter just laughed and said that he sure did take good care of her.

One evening Walter, Tom, and I were sitting on the shop porch talking. Walter saw three women walking down the road toward us. As they approached, Walter and Tom recognized them as a mother and her two daughters who worked as prostitutes in Bryson City. Walter went across the road and talked with the women for a few minutes. Then the women continued down the road. Walter returned to the shop and said, "Let's go." Walter and Tom trailed off after the women.

They were gone for a little while, and when they returned they asked me why I had not followed them. They said that they went down by the river and waited, saving the thirteen-year-old girl for me. I told them that I was not interested and let it go at that. They thought I was just plain dumb.

Two or three years later I heard that Walter had cancer, and I went to his house to see him. I found him lying in his bed. He had recently had his right leg amputated up near the hip. He was in good spirits, but he died shortly after my visit.

Later Tom would take a job at the Cherokee Boy's Club. That's where he worked until he retired. Years later I came across a death announcement for Tom's son in the *Cherokee One Feather*. The announcement referred to Tom as Reverend. I guess that, similar to many Indians, Tom took up preaching later in life.

Philip, Grandma's youngest child, was not the most motivated person I have known. He lived at home until around
1940, when he married Gladys, and as far as I remember, he
never had a regular job until he joined the navy. After the
Second World War Philip returned to Cherokee and built
a four-room shack up the road from Grandma's house on
Kate Lambert Branch, just below Grandma's spring. Philip
bought a big flatbed log truck and started hauling logs.
This business was competitive, and it was hard for drivers
to make much money, so to supplement his income, Philip
took up preaching. During the summer he would drive his
big truck around the reservation to haul people to his revivals. More than once I found myself riding along.

In 1949, short of money, Philip sold Grandma's old house
and fifteen acres of road frontage to Dad for fifteen hundred dollars. This was the land Dad purchased just before
we moved to Mars Hill. Philip kept his old house and about
six acres. For a few years Philip and his family continued
to live in Grandma Kate's old house. Then in 1951, when
Dad and I built the gift shop in front of the old Kate Lambert house, Philip moved his family back up the branch to
his old house.

One summer in the early 1950s, when Mom and I were
operating the gift shop, Philip needed more money and sold
his pasture to Dad for $125. Dad, knowing that Philip was
desperate, paid Philip before the contract papers had been
drawn up. After the sale Dad kept asking Philip to draw up
the papers on the land transfer, but Philip kept delaying.

Mom and I thought that we owned the land, so we decided to buy a few cattle, fatten them in the pastures during the summer, and then sell them in the fall. We were going to make a lot of money. We went ahead and hired a couple of guys to clear the pasture. As soon as we sent the workers up to clear the pasture, Gladys barreled out of her house and ordered them off the land.

When they came back to the shop and told Mom what had happened, Mom's left eyebrow rose to her hairline. This meant that she was really pissed off. Mom bolted out of the shop in a flurry and went up the dirt road to confront Gladys. By the time she got to the path to Gladys's house, Gladys was already waiting in her front yard. Mom asked Gladys what business she had running our workers off our land. Mom was really in a tough mood. Gladys, in a tougher mood, told Mom that Philip had not sold the land to Dad. She said that Philip had only borrowed the money. Then Gladys had the nerve to order Mom off her property. Well, Mom, madder than an old wet setting hen, spun around, left the path, and came back down to the shop.

Mom never did like Gladys, and sometimes Mom said some nasty things about her—once she asserted that someone other than Philip had fathered a couple of Philip's children while Philip was away in the navy. While Mom was standing there in the shop, she was not just mad, she was furious enough to make that claim again, along with a few other even more unsavory comments about Gladys. After a long, long time Mom finally simmered down.

That evening we waited for Philip to come home. We were hoping that Philip would say it was just a misunderstanding. But I knew Philip: I really did not expect him to say that. When Philip came by the shop on the way home, we flagged him down and told him what had happened. Philip cleared up the matter, all right. He told us that he had not sold the land. Then he just threw his head back, laughed his famous loud laugh, and went on his happy way up the road to his house. Now I was mad. Dejected, Mom and I decided that there was no doubt that we had been done out of $125. We decided that Dad had been dumb for not suspecting that his own brother would cheat him like this.

A couple of days later, before Dad came home for the weekend, Philip pulled his big log truck into our parking lot, got out of his truck, walked into the shop, threw $125 on the counter, and walked out, once again throwing back his head and laughing his big loud laugh. Mom and I were happy to have the money, but we really wanted the land. As far as I was concerned, Dad was off the hook, but not so for Mom, and boy, did she give him a chewing out when he arrived home for the weekend. I never spoke to Philip again, nor did I ever ride with him again to one of his revivals. I never saw him save another soul.

At the end of my first summer running the shop, just before I was due to begin my studies at Mars Hill College, I was not feeling well. I closed the shop and returned to Mars Hill. Then I went to the doctor to find out why I felt so sick. He took one look at me and said that I had a mild case of hepatitis. I think I contracted the disease by swimming in the Oconaluftee River. He sent me home and ordered me to go to bed and to eat plenty of sweets. I followed his orders, and about a month later I was well enough to start classes at Mars Hill College.

I enrolled at Mars Hill College, in part, to save my life. On June 25, 1950, North Korea invaded South Korea, and President Truman responded by deploying our troops. This time the U.S. government did not call the engagement a war; instead they referred to it as a police action. But it was a war. Over one hundred thousand American soldiers were wounded and thirty thousand killed. When I entered college, all eighteen-year-old men were subject to the draft, and I, like my father before me, was determined to postpone my entry into the military as long as possible. I decided that my best option for avoiding the conflict was to stay in school and use the educational deferment. Any college student could obtain a deferment from the draft during their first year of college. If you placed yourself in the upper half of your freshman class, you could extend this deferment for the remaining three years. The hitch was that when you accepted the deferment, you were almost guaranteed to be drafted at the end of four years of college, regardless of whether or not you had finished. After I entered college, I obtained my deferment, and I worked hard to make sure that I graduated no later than 1955, when my deferment expired.

Even though I started school late, I had no trouble catching up in all my classes. I enrolled in pre-engineering, and under the guidance of "Pop" Lance I did well. Lance was a lay preacher, an old-fashioned professor, and a former football coach. He told us many stories about his view of life. He impressed me.

I slid effortlessly into the social life of the college, and I was not unlike any other student. Bill and I became fast friends with one of the lead singers in the musicals that the drama department staged. He had a magnificent voice. He was older, maybe twenty-three, a veteran sailor, and had many stories to tell about the places he had visited. He had visited Havana several times and had delightful stories to tell about his time in the Cuban bars. He was much more worldly than we were, a trait that I am sure made him attractive to the college voice coach, whom he would end up marrying.

Bill, the former sailor, and I joined one of the college's literary societies. We met once a week, and during the meetings parliamentary procedure was strictly observed. Anyone who broke a rule was fined. At meetings we read and held practice sessions for our evening serenades of the women students. After our meeting ended, we would march to the women's dorms, where we stood under the dorm windows and sang the love songs of the great Mario Lanza. The women would hang out their windows, in their nightgowns, thrilled by the former sailor's magnificent voice. We would sing a couple of songs at each dorm and then head to the donut shop for a late-night snack.

I realized that I was lucky to be a day student who could go home each evening and escape the overbearing rules of the college and the vigilant eyes of the housemothers. The college administration made it their business to keep the students occupied, and they did a good job at it. After all, as they saw it, an idle mind is the devil's workshop. All the students went to church Sunday evenings. Wednesday evenings offered prayer meetings. Tuesday, Thursday, and Saturday evenings offered movies at the auditorium. They also expected students to behave as adults at all times, and Dean Lee dealt sternly with students who didn't live up to the college's standards. The dean enforced a demerit system. Any student who accumulated fifty demerits in one semester was expelled. The dean made sure that that any infraction would place a student in peril. For instance, if a faculty member saw a boy and girl kissing, or a student smoking, the dean immediately assigned forty-nine and one half demerits. The dean awarded fifty demerits to any student who was caught drinking alcohol. This disciplinary policy was very strict, and as a result there were few problem students at the college.

Still, before they came to Mars Hill, some students had spent all their short lives closely supervised by their parents, and they thought that they would be free once they arrived on campus. They quickly learned, however, that at Mars Hill College they would be supervised much more closely than they ever had been at home. At Mars Hill a boy could not even hold a girl's hand without being in danger of accruing demerits. A private, quiet moment with a girl in a dark place was out of the question. Even though they had no hope of seducing anyone, these boys still harbored desires that they bantered about during nightly bull sessions.

One night some of the older boys who were listening in on a bull session decided that some of these frustrated freshmen were ripe targets. A college prayer house was located in a large patch of woods on the hilltop behind the college barn. This prayer house was a shack where students could go to meditate or hold prayer meetings. A large patch of blackberry briars lay between a clear pasture and the woods that extended up to shack.

A couple of guys in our class told a couple of the naive younger students that an old man lived in the house on top of the hill with his young, beautiful, sex-starved teenage daughter. They added that the old man went out every night, left his daughter alone, and did not return until long after midnight. The naive boys took the bait and said that they wanted to visit the girl while the father was out. The older boys assured the freshmen that they could arrange a meeting.

On the designated night one of the tricksters hid in the cabin with a shotgun. At around nine the boys eagerly crept along the hilltop trail to the cabin. As they neared the cabin, they noticed a dim light in the window, and they imagined the young girl sitting there impatiently waiting for them. They tapped on the door and waited. Then the door flung open, only to reveal a bearded old man brandishing a shotgun. Pointing the gun in the boy's direction, the old man yelled, "So you are the sons-of-bitches who have been messing around with my daughter." The boys, frightened to death, ran frantically into the darkness as the old man shot the gun into the air. The boys headed down the hill toward the barn and ran smack into the briar patch. They did not slow down until they came to the barn near the main highway, by which time the briars had scratched up every inch of their exposed skin. They returned to the dormitory and patched themselves up as best they could. By the next morning the story had spread throughout the school, and every girl snickered as the boys passed by. The boys were the laughingstock of the school.

Mars Hill College was then a good two-year liberal arts college, and I credit this school with having given me the confidence that I could become a college graduate. After my first year at Mars Hill College a few of the other engineering students and I decided that another year at Mars Hill would be a waste of time. The next autumn Bill Edwards and I moved to Raleigh and enrolled in the school of engineering at North Carolina State College. There is no question that my decision to leave the mountains and go to State was the right one, but still it was a decision my mother found difficult to accept.

I could not come to Cherokee in the summer of 1954 because North Carolina State required each engineering student to work in their field of study during the summer between their junior and senior years. Along with three other classmates I had landed a choice summer job in Raleigh with Carolina Power and Light. I liked the work and made good money. My mother, however, had other plans.

During that summer my sister Betty and her husband, Bruce, were running our gift shop in Cherokee. In the first week of August Mom called and told me to quit my job and return to Cherokee to help her run the shop. I tried my best to beg off, but Mom insisted that I return. She said that Betty and Bruce had to start classes by mid-August. I gave in, quit my job, returned to Cherokee, and helped Mom close out the season. This was the most miserable month of my life. Mom had always been mean, but that August she outdid herself. She never had a pleasant word to say. To make matters worse, every now and then she would get mad over nothing, come at me scratching and clawing, and beat the hell out of me. I would just stand there and take it. Her tantrums would come on without warning, as if she were suppressing some great hatred of me that would erupt now and then. Maybe she was just mad at the world in general, and I was the only one around to take her abuse. I have always tried to figure out why she was so ornery that summer. Maybe she was mad at me for going away to school in Raleigh.

Going off to North Carolina State was probably the best decision I ever made, if only because it was there that I met Julia Drake. In the summer of 1955 I had to take a few summer school classes to complete my degree so that I could graduate in August of that year. One summer evening Phil Reese and I were cruising around town in his Mercury. We came upon a group of girls sitting on the sidewalk steps

on a street near Five Points in Raleigh. We stopped to talk
with them, and it was there that I met Julia. I took her to
a movie, *Strategic Air Command*, staring Jimmy Stewart and
June Allyson, and from there we started spending more
time together.

After I graduated in 1955 I accepted a job with the Tennessee Valley Authority in Chattanooga, Tennessee. Before
I started that job I went to Mars Hill to visit my parents for
a week and found myself working on a one-week appoint-
ment for the college in Dad's maintenance crew. The afternoon of the first day we were to dig up a sewer line near
one of the men's dorms. When we arrived at the site, Dad
informed the crew that the sewer was backed up under the
dorm. This meant that we would have to crawl up under
the dorm to work in that stench, and we crew members began eyeing each other, wondering who would be the lucky
one to land the first shift. I quickly learned that Dad had
me in mind for the job. I crouched down and looked under the building, and all I could think was that here I was
with a brand-new electrical engineering degree, and I was
getting ready to crawl into a filthy three-foot-high crawl
space filled with spiderwebs to dig a ditch. After looking
into the void for a while, I rose, looked around, and told
Dad that Mom had a lot of beans to can and that I wanted
to help her. If Dad wanted to use me, his newly minted college graduate son, to look good in the eyes of his workers,
he failed. I turned and walked down the hill toward home
and never looked back.

I was not in Chattanooga working for the TVA long before I received my draft notice. I went home for Thanksgiving, and then on the seventh of December Dad put me on the bus for Knoxville so that I could report for duty. There two men in uniform led us around. First we took the written test, which was simple, probably at a second-grade level. Only one of us, a boy from Hot Springs, a small town deep in the mountains, managed to fail. After the written tests we were led into a room and ordered to strip to our shorts for the physical exam. While we undressed, our two escorts were betting each other how many of us wore boxers and how many wore jockey shorts. They laughed when they saw that the boy from Hot Springs wore no shorts at all. When the physical exam was done, we were led into a room and told to face the flag. When the boy from Hot Springs tried to enter, they told him to wait outside. Then a bored officer came into the room and swore us into the army.

We spent the night in Knoxville, and the next morning we were put on a bus for basic training in Fort Jackson, South Carolina. On the way to Fort Jackson the bus stopped in Hot Springs, and the driver told the boy without shorts to get off. The boy asked the driver if this meant he was not going to get to go into the army. The driver did not answer directly but simply said that he would be back sometime to pick him up and the army would let him know when. The boy nodded and looked very disappointed as he got off the bus. All of us on the bus felt sorry for the boy because he wanted so much to join the army. I think that

I felt particularly sorry for the boy because I understood how easily I could have been in his position.

After basic training at Fort Jackson, South Carolina, I married Julia on February 19. From there the army sent me to Fort Monmouth, New Jersey, for specialized training and then to Fort Huachuca in Arizona, where I assisted in testing advanced radar systems. This is where our first son, Bob, was born in 1957. When I completed my tour of duty, I returned to North Carolina, where I landed a job with ALCOA at the Calderwood Dam. My second son, Michael, was born in 1960 while we were living there. A couple of years later I was transferred to the ALCOA offices in Maryville.

At Maryville I spent a lot of time providing tours to visitors who wanted to see the dams, lakes, and powerhouses. One morning Mead Warren, my big boss, told me that I was to take Ben Sloan, a smelter department manager from the Pittsburgh office, on a tour of the watershed. I met Ben at around nine in the morning, and we headed out to the car for the trip to the mountains. Ben was very large man, and he had trouble getting into the Chevrolet Corvair. Once he was snugly seated in the car, I took him through all the powerhouses, ending up, as I usually did on these tours, at Tapoco Lodge for lunch.

On the return trip we stopped at the Calderwood Lake overlook, where we got out of the car to admire the beautiful lake below. We stood there talking when Ben, quite unexpectedly, asked me what I wanted to do during my career with ALCOA. The question caught me off-guard. To be honest, I had never given any thought to my long-term goals, and I told him that I was perfectly happy working in the Maryville power department as a power engineer. I am sure that Ben was disappointed. Now I know that he wanted me to say that I wanted to come to Pittsburgh, work for him, and eventually become an officer in the corporate office. In the years to come I would meet many people in the corporate office who were just like Ben. Managers at his level all seemed to believe that every young engineer aspired to reach that level as well. I have to admit that as I became more acquainted with the corporate structure, I too aspired to climb the ladder of corporate success. But it only took a couple of years on the first rung to convince me that life would be much more enjoyable if I just forgot that ladder and jumped at every opportunity the job presented to travel.

When I started working for Alcoa, I might have thought that I would spend my career working on dams near Cherokee, but that quickly changed. I was not in Maryville long before I found myself transferred out of the mountains, north to Pittsburgh. Just a few years after meeting Ben Sloan, Julia, the children, and I were in Suriname, South America. From there ALCOA sent me to projects throughout the world. My daughter, Carol, would be born in Pittsburgh in 1968, during one of my many assignments to the corporate headquarters. My twenty-five-year career with the Aluminum Company would take me to, among other places, Suriname, Australia, Brazil, and Mexico. Later I would work for other companies in India and Korea. While growing up as a poor Indian child in Birdtown, it was beyond my imagination that, sixty years later, I would have the opportunity to visit over sixty countries.

All my siblings were able to attend college. Sibbald, Betty, and I graduated. This is quite remarkable in light of the fact that I never once remember my parents having really expected us to do so. I can only conclude that it was Mom and Dad's intense focus on having money that inspired us to succeed. Betty married Bruce Hawkins, a dentist who had a very successful practice near Charlotte in Mt. Holly. Sibbald graduated from the University of Tennessee and then worked in the textile industry for several years, after which he became a preacher. He worked as a preacher in Weaverville, North Carolina, and Spruce Pine, also in North Carolina. Don studied at the University of Tennessee as well and worked as an industrial engineer for Martin-Marietta. Helen married Joe Brown, who was operating his parents' dairy farm at that time. Joe gave up farming, studied piloting, and became a copilot on a corporate airplane. After Joe died of cancer in 1990, Helen married Lewis Harding, a retired pilot, who is also enrolled in the Eastern Band. After he retired from the airline business, Lew returned to Cherokee and worked selflessly in many capacities to advance the economic and political interests of the tribe. Notably, he currently serves as chair of the Cherokee Historical Association, as a member of the Tribal Casino Gaming Enterprise board, and as commander of the American Legion post in Cherokee.

As for Dad, around 1961 he took a leave of absence from his job at Mars Hill College to build a restaurant on his nine-acre property located on Route 19 in Soco Valley on the reservation. After the construction Dad returned to Mars Hill and learned that his job had been given to someone else. He and Mom moved back to Cherokee, into Grandma Lambert's old house in Birdtown. In 1966 they moved from there into a singlewide trailer Dad had installed behind their restaurant in Soco.

Dad got a job with the tribe building the nature trail located just above the Oconaluftee Indian Village. This was his pride and joy. Mom and Dad continued to farm. They tended a small garden, a field of blueberry bushes, some chickens, and a few head of cattle. In the 1970s Dad built a small house behind his trailer, where Mom and Dad would live out their days. A few years later Don, Betty, and Sibbald purchased some of Dad's road-front property and built a simple motel that they named, quite simply, The Homestead. Today the motel is owned and operated by Helen and Lewis.

After Dad moved into his house in Soco, my uncle Willard was arrested for a couple of serious infractions. When he was seventy the federal authorities, using aircraft, discovered a marijuana crop on his little farm on Adams Creek. He grew and harvested the marijuana, baled it, and stored it in his barn like hay until he could sell it. He was tried in the federal court in Asheville, and because of his age and the fact that he was a poor Indian, the judge fined him only five thousand dollars.

Sometime later the park rangers arrested him for game poaching in the Great Smoky Mountains National Park. He and a couple of his sons, who were avid hunters, drove into the park one night in search of a bear or a deer. They drove slowly while scanning the woods with a spotlight. On this particular night the rangers had set up some deer decoys along the road at the edge of the woods in an attempt to catch poachers. When Willard saw the decoys, he stopped the car, got out, and started shooting. The rangers promptly arrested him and his sons. Again he and his sons were tried in the federal court. The court fined them and banned them from entering the park. He was lucky to have escaped serving time for his offenses.

Just before Willard died of lung cancer, Dad and I went to visit him. We drove into his front yard, where his children and their families were sitting or standing around waiting for Willard to die. While we were standing on Willard's front porch, Dad said, "Isn't it wonderful that Willard can sit on this porch, look down Adams Creek, and see all his children's houses?" I repeated after him, "Wonderful." To be honest, I did not really feel that it was wonderful. I wondered who in their right mind would want to live all their lives on Adams Creek or, for that matter, in sight of their parents' front porch. I think that none of Willard's children ever moved off the reservation. That said, I did meet two of his great-grandsons, Jason and Damon Lambert, while they were studying at the University of North Carolina at

Chapel Hill. Today both work for the tribe in significant positions, Daman as transportation planner and Jason as director of economic development.

After this little conversation Dad and I went into the front room and found Willard lying on a bed by the window, in a semicoma. He did not even know we were there. Willard would sort of come out of the coma and move around a bit as he continually tried to reach his pack of cigarettes and lighter that lay on the windowsill by his bed. As he lay dying, Willard was not about to give up his cigarettes.

As for Dad, he died of leukemia in January 1993. Dad knew he was dying and told everyone that he just wanted to hang on long enough to see the flowers bloom. One day I was sitting in the living room of his home with him when he said, "Did you see that?" I said, "See what?" It seemed to me that the only thing he could see from where he was sitting was his television. He said that he had just seen the most beautiful field of purple azaleas and then asked again if I had seen it as well. Again I told him that I could not see them. A few days later he was gone.

Mom struggled on after Dad died, but her health declined rapidly. She became very difficult as we attempted to deal with her for her own welfare. Soon she was not able to care for herself, and in 2000 we had to place her in a nursing home over the mountain from Cherokee, in Waynesville. Pneumonia put her on death's doorstep a couple of times. Then it looked like she was going to slip away on October 10, 2002. Everyone was notified, but she regained consciousness a couple of days later. Once again it looked like she was going to pull through. My siblings were there with her the day she came back around. She told them that she wanted to go home. They asked her if she meant that she wanted to go back to her home in Cherokee. She said, "No, not there. I want to go home." In the wee hours of the following morning Mom was gone.

Mom's funeral service was held in Sylva at Moody Funeral Home, right in the shadow of the same courthouse where she and Dad had gotten married seventy years earlier. From there the procession made the trek to the Mars Hill Cemetery, where eight of her grandsons carried her to her final resting place adjacent to Dad's grave, right next to the grave of Dr. Otis Duck, our next-door neighbor when we lived in a three-room shack in Mars Hill. The Mars Hill Cemetery is located atop a picturesque hill overlooking the Mars Hill town and countryside. This is where Mom's sister Helen and her husband, Boyd, are also buried.

For many reasons Mom was proud of her grandsons who carried her to her final resting place. Looking back, it is remarkable how far this Lambert family has come from the humble beginnings of a sixteen-year-old bride and her twenty-three-year-old husband. Neither Leonard Sr. nor Carrie had much of an education. Early on they made their living from the land and began their married life in a one-room log cabin on an Indian reservation. Mom and Dad left five children and fifteen grandchildren. Of these children, grandchildren, and their spouses, thirty-three earned bachelor's degrees, three earned master's degrees, and three earned doctorates. Professionally, Mom and Dad left behind a family that included a physician, a dentist, a lawyer, an architect, several engineers, and two professors. I have to say that the Sylva Courthouse had reason to stand so proud after all.

Equally impressive is how much the Eastern Band of Cherokees has changed during this period. In the 1930s the reservation was an economic backwater almost entirely dependent on the benevolence of the federal government. The living conditions in Cherokee have certainly improved since I was a child growing up in the cove. Still, the stuck-in-the-1950s feel of the reservation has not entirely given way. The hand-built wood and log homes of my childhood have been replaced with mobile homes and red brick HUD homes. Despite the tribe's revitalization program there is still some Indian kitsch—oversized teepees, wood Indians (in Western Plains garb), ubiquitous tomahawks, and other paraphernalia the Cherokees historically never used—that gaudily adorns downtown Cherokee shops and many of the reservation motels. The visitors to gift shops and so-called galleries can find plenty of trinkets and things, pure junk, most of which is made in China. Much of it the same junk I sold in my gift shop so many years before.

One of my classmates at Birdtown School was "Chief" Henry Lambert, the world's most photographed Indian. He spent his days dressed in magnificent Western Indian garb, standing in front of his buffalo-skin teepee, waiting for a tourist to pay him five dollars to take his photo. One day he explained to me that he had tried wearing traditional Cherokee dress, but the tourists just were not interested. They did not want the simple Cherokee dress; they did not want to see a real Indian. They wanted to see an Indian who looked like a Hollywood Indian and matched what they thought an Indian should look like. He said that once he started wearing a Sioux headdress, his business took off. Look at Chief Henry's photo on one of the Cherokee post-cards, and you will see a decorative Indian that should satisfy every dim-witted tourist's taste. Chief Henry happily fed their desires and took his earnings, and I would guess that he used them to pay his kids' way through college. It seems that this strategy worked, as one of his sons went on to earn a law degree, after which he returned to Cherokee and became a major player in tribal politics.

The Cherokee tourist trade boomed in the 1950s and 1960s. However, in the 1970s the tourist industry waned, and the tribe's attempt to attract small industry failed. At the same time, in the 1970s, the tribe opened a very large bingo parlor that offered a one-hundred-thousand-dollar pot each month. Apparently the parlor was very successful, but we rarely saw the impact of this revenue. Perhaps someone stole the proceeds.

In 1997 the Eastern Band of Cherokees opened a casino, and the tribe moved into a new era. Today the town of Cherokee is the vibrant economic heart of western North Carolina, with a gaming and tourism industry that generates over three hundred million dollars of revenue per year. This new wealth has integrated the Eastern Band ever more deeply into the western North Carolina economy and simultaneously has ushered in an area of ever more political and financial independence. In addition this wealth has had a very positive effect on the lives of many non-Indians living throughout western North Carolina. In part due to the wealth that the casino generates, the tribe has been able to assume greater control over its destiny and can now begin to shake itself free from dependence on the paternal social programs of the federal government and even try to reclaim from Hollywood some of the more offensive Indian imagery. I think that it would be fair to say that, arguably, today the tribe is more financially secure and politically powerful than it has ever been in its five-hundred-year history. Over the years this small band of Indians has faced many challenges and has persevered even when many tribal members wanted to yield their right to the North Carolina land in return for a small government handout.

As I think about the tribal leaders' steadfastness in holding the land, I sometimes wonder what influenced them to stand firm in the face of the sometimes strong opposition. You may accuse me of being a romantic; however, I think that our ancestors, when facing these dilemmas, looked up at the hills surrounding Cherokee and decided that they just could not even consider giving up their homeland. With reason I think the 121st Psalm is a good touchstone for the Eastern Band. I know the psalm is a point of reference for me. I remember very well the first time I attended the Eastern Band presentation of the outdoor drama *Unto These Hills*. Kermit Hunter did himself very well when he incorporated this psalm into the beginning of the performance. I remember it was sometime in 1951 that we were all sitting there in the Mountainside Theater as the night darkness began to replace the fading twilight. Then Mr. Underwood, the drama's orator, spoke the opening lines of the psalm. Shivers went up my spine as I heard him say, "I will lift up mine eyes unto the hills, from whence cometh my help."

After that performance this psalm became my favorite. When I was born we faced the perils of hunger, lack of clothing, and the dangers of disease that lived in the valleys and hills of the Boundary. Now I look back fondly to those days with satisfaction and pride that my mother and father, similar to other Eastern Cherokees and non-Indians in the area, worked hard and built our family on firm foundations in the valleys of these hills.

Yes, all one need do is lift up one's eyes . . .

Notes

Forethoughts

1. Gore Vidal, *Palimpsest: A Memoire* (New York: Penguin Books, 1996).

2. 30 U.S. (5 Pet.) 1, 8 L. Ed. 25 (1831); 31 U.S. (6 Pet.) 515, 8 L. Ed. 483 (1832).

3. An Eastern Cherokee is an enrolled member and citizen of the Eastern Band of Cherokee Indians.

4. Vine Deloria, *Custer Died for Your Sins* (New York: Macmillan, 1969), 82.

5. The reservation of the Eastern Band of Cherokee Indians is often referred to by Eastern Cherokees as the Qualla Boundary, or simply "the Boundary." In *The Eastern Band of Cherokee Indians, 1819–1900* (Knoxville: University of Tennessee Press, 1984) John Finger suggests that this usage dates to at least 1850, well before the Eastern Band had been recognized by the U.S. Congress as a distinct tribe in 1868 (51). The term "Boundary" references the fact that these lands did not originate as a reservation for the Eastern Cherokee. Rather, after the Cherokees were dispossessed of their land following the removal, the Eastern Cher-

okee purchased the land of the Boundary. To this day this fact informs the way in which Eastern Cherokees understand their relationship to the Boundary.

6. The hoop dance has been historically performed by the Indians of the American Southwest, not the Southeast. See Kurt Dombrowski, *Against Culture: Development, Politics and Religion in Indian Alaska* (Lincoln: University of Nebraska Press, 2001); Michelene Pesantubbee, "Culture Revitalization and Indigenization of Churches among the Choctaw of Oklahoma" (PhD diss., University of Oklahoma, 1994). Both Dombrowski and Pesantubbee have documented a similar response among Christian Indians to so-called traditional beliefs in Alaska and Oklahoma, respectively.

7. These "chiefs" should not be confused with the principal chief of the Eastern Band of Cherokee Indians. The principal chief is the highest political official of the Eastern Band and is elected to this office by the members of the tribe. The chiefs referred to here do not hold a position in the tribal government.

8. I thank my colleague Eunice Sahel for this wonderful term. To my knowledge "anthropologize" was first used in this way by Paul Rabinow in his article "Representations Are Social Facts: Modernity and Post-Modernity in Anthropology," in *Writing Culture*, ed. James Clifford and George Marcus (Berkeley: University of California Press, 1986). Regrettably, it has not entered the common lexicon of anthropologists.

9. Wilbur G. Zeigler and Ben S. Grosscup, *The Heart of the Alleghenies or Western North Carolina* (Raleigh NC: Alfred Williams and Co., 1883), 36.

Roots

1. Peggy Lambert of Cherokee NC generously made a copy of the story that Sibbald Smith wrote available to me.

2. Ordered to be assembled by the U.S. Court of Claims in

1906, the Guion-Miller Roll was designed to be a definitive list of the descendants of all Cherokees east of the Mississippi who were listed on the 1835 removal census and who had not been removed to Indian Territory.

3. The treaty of 1819 provided reservations of 640 acres to Cherokees who agreed to renounce their citizenship in the Cherokee Nation. This treaty also moved the boundary between the Cherokee Nation and the United States south of Quallatown. Among others many Quallatown Cherokees accepted this offer. After they lost their reservations to claims made by North Carolina, some of these Quallatown Cherokees remained in Quallatown; others moved south and back into the Cherokee Nation. See Finger, *Eastern Band of Cherokees*, 11.

4. The story of Tsali has been widely told. James Mooney made it famous in *Myths of the Cherokee* (1900; New York: Dover Publications, 1995), 131, 157–58. Finger presents the most detailed scholarly account in *Eastern Band of Cherokees*, 21–28. Charles Frazer fictionalized it in his novel *Thirteen Moons* (New York: Random House, 2006). And it is the climactic moment of the outdoor drama *Unto These Hills*, performed during the summer in Cherokee at the Mountainside Theater. Matthew Thompson has explored the changing place of Tsali in this outdoor drama in his unpublished paper "Another Crossroads on the Horizon: Three Narratives of the Past and More to Come as the Eastern Band Cherokee Rewrite Their History for Tourists and Themselves," presented at the American Studies Association annual conference, Albuquerque, Oct. 16–19, 2008.

5. Finger, *Eastern Band of Cherokees*, 18.

6. For a discussion of Evan Jones see William Gerald McLoughlin, Walter H. Conser, and Virginia Duffy McLoughlin, *The Cherokee Ghost Dance: Essays on the Southeastern Indians, 1789–1861* (Macon GA: Mercer University Press, 1984); William Gerald McLoughlin,

After the Trail of Tears: The Cherokees' Struggle for Sovereignty, 1839–1880 (Raleigh: University of North Carolina Press, 1993); William G. McLoughlin, *The Cherokees and Christianity, 1794–1870* (Athens: University of Georgia Press, 2008).

7. Finger, *Eastern Band of Cherokees*, 86.

8. Finger, *Eastern Band of Cherokees*, 86.

9. Finger, *Eastern Band of Cherokees*, 155, 175.

10. Finger, *Eastern Band of Cherokees*, 157.

11. Finger, *Eastern Band of Cherokees*, 157.

12. L. G. Moses, *The Indian Man: A Biography of James Mooney* (Urbana: University of Illinois Press, 1984), 85. Moses's account of this incident includes two minor errors. First, he incorrectly spells Sibbald's name "Sibbold." Second, he says that Mary Smith was Nimrod Jarrett Smith's sister-in-law. In fact she was his wife and, at the time of this incident, his widow. James Mooney, the author of the classic *Myths of the Cherokee*, was invited to conduct research in Cherokee by Chief Jarrett Smith. They met at the Smithsonian Institution during one of Chief Smith's official visits to Washington DC.

13. John Finger, *Cherokee Americans: The Eastern Band of Cherokees in the Twentieth Century* (Lincoln: University of Nebraska Press, 1991), 48–50, 66. Following the removal their legal status was a lingering issue for the Eastern Cherokees. Although they had renounced their citizenship in the Cherokee Nation, they had not been guaranteed citizenship by the state of North Carolina. The Eastern Cherokees were possibly the last group of people who were born in the United States to have their right to U.S. citizenship guaranteed by law. This was achieved through an act of Congress in 1930. Even following the passage of this act, resistance remained among non-Indians in western North Carolina to the ability of the Eastern Cherokees to exercise their rights of citizenship.

14. In the early years of the twentieth century the U.S. government was attempting to deal with the "Indian problem" by dissolving tribal governments and allocating tribal assets to individual tribal members. The Baker Roll was assembled in preparation of the dissolution of the Eastern Band as part of this project. After the project of dissolving the tribe was abandoned, the Baker Roll became the base roll for membership in the tribe. See Finger, *Cherokee Americans*, 47–52.

15. For the story of Alexander Cumming's journey see William Steele, *The Cherokee Crown of Tannassy* (Winston-Salem NC: J. F. Blair Publisher, 1977).

The Cove

1. In the *Farmer's Almanac* each astrological sign is associated with a body part. The "feet sign" is Pisces.

2. While this characterization of the end of Quaker schools in Cherokee reveals much about my father's view of tribal politics, it greatly simplifies a complicated and nuanced series of events. The battle for control of the schools was bitter, protracted, and implicated in national party politics as well as local tribal politics. For a more complete discussion of the unfolding of these events see Finger, *Eastern Band of Cherokees*, 150–58.